Hormones… The Movie! (Screenplay)
Copyright © 2021 Rolfe Kanefsky. All Rights Reserved.

No portion of this publication may be reproduced, stored, and/or copied electronically (except for academic use as a source), nor transmitted in any form or by any means without the prior written permission of the publisher and/or author.

Published in the USA by
BearManor Media
1317 Edgewater Dr. #110
Orlando, FL 32804
www.BearManorMedia.com

Softcover Edition
ISBN: 978-1-62933-757-9

Printed in the United States of America

THE WORLD OF THE TEEN SEX COMEDY

A Forward to "HORMONES… The Screenplay! By Rolfe Kanefsky

What you are about to read is my unproduced teen comedy screenplay entitled, "HORMONES...The Movie!" Now in order to put this script and the whole genre into perspective, one needs to go back to a more innocent time, or some might say, a more "socially unacceptable" time, the 1980s! Stories and writers to some extent are a product of their time. They are influenced by world events and their surroundings and can be influencers as well. Before things became too "P.C." or we "woke" up, comedies were able to tread on grounds that today are considered dangerous. Mel Brooks has said that his comedy classic "**Blazing Saddles**" made in 1974 could never be made today. Same could be said for many great films of the past. Because of the time they were made, some of these films can be "forgiven" and still accepted and appreciated as great comedies. Other films date very badly. Comedy can depend on the environment it takes place in. About two years ago I went to a special screening of the Patrick Swayze's flick "**Road House**" made in 1989. The audience had a great time but all admitted that you could never make this film now due to today's "climate". So how does one begin to discuss the world of "exploitation cinema" that sometimes overlaps into "sexploitation cinema" without offending someone? Basically, the answer is, you can't. Someone will always find something to get upset about because comedy is in the eye of the beholder. What's hysterical to one is gross and disgusting to another. A beautiful nude body can be appreciated and at the same time attacked by people who find nudity offensive. This is especially true in America where sex sells but if you look at it you're called a pervert. Hormones be damned! Arousal is evil thanks to some religions. But if you're told you can't see something, you want to see it even more, especially if you're a boy or girl going through puberty but I digress.

So, let's jump now to 1987 when I went to Hampshire college. I took a film course and made a short horror film called, "**Just Listen**". A piece of this film is seen in the beginning of my first feature film, "**There's Nothing Out There**". In the short, a college girl has a fight with her boyfriend, goes into the woods, smokes some pot, finds a dead body, gets attacked by a male killer, fights him off and gets away. However, she starts seeing visions of him everywhere that quickly drive her crazy and she ends up killing her boyfriend, thinking he's the killer. When I showed this film in my film class, some of the female students were offended by the short. They didn't like the woman being the victim and then becoming the killer. My response was that this is a horror film and in a horror film, the lead women really can only be a victim or a killer or if you don't put any women in the film like in John Carpenter's masterpiece "**The Thing**", then you get criticized for not having enough roles for women. They couldn't really argue with me after that statement.

In many ways, the same can be said for teen comedies. There is a formula to the genre and it is very simple. Horny boys trying to get laid. That's the basic premise of 99.9% of these comedies as either the driving force of the story or a subplot or multiple subplots. If you are going to see a film like "Porky's" or "**American Pie**", you should know what you're in for. If you are not a fan of this genre, then don't watch the movies. Since most of these films are from the guy's point of view, women are the love or lust objects in the film. Nobody is reinventing the wheel when it comes to teen sex comedies. Many of them are crude, rude, blatantly UN-P.C. and were enjoyed at a time before the internet when seeing a "naked woman" was a big deal for boys who have recently gone through puberty. These films were devoured mostly by 12-18 year old males. They were funny and silly with just enough bare flesh on screen to satisfy their intended audiences. And in the 1980's, they were kings at the box office! Almost all of them were rated "R" and that was the stamp of approval which promised they would be naughty enough to tease and titillate the male fans who were 17 years and older.

Even the films that are now regarded as classics like "**Fast Times At Ridgemont High**", "**Risky Business**", "**Revenge Of The Nerds**", "**Bachelor Party**", and "**Porky's**" all provided laughs and beautiful naked women such as Phoebe Cates, Rebecca De Mornay, Kim Cattrall, and Monique Gabrielle. They sometimes called these comedies "Coming Of Age" films and for very good reason. Emphasis on the "coming". That bad pun is a prime example of the level of humor in most of these films.

So, that brings me to my influences growing up before I wrote "Hormones...The Movie!" I was born in 1969 so as the 1980s hit so did my sex drive. This was also the rise of VHS and the home video market. Now pornography was obviously around but we weren't inundated with it like today on home computers. My sexual awakening came at a more innocent time. I found my father's Playboy magazines, got to see some "R" rated films on cable television. Films like the Charlie Band produced softcore musical "**Cinderella**" probably scarred me for life. One never quite forgets the idea of a "snapping pussy" or a woman having sex with a corncob until popcorn is shooting out of her crotch. Yes, there were some weird movies made in the late 70s/early 80s. And when it came to renting, nobody really checked I.D. ages in Ma & Pa video stores. So, I rented a lot of teen comedies and horror flicks growing up. Both of which had their share of female flesh on display. Most movies were available to watch and enjoy. When I got my first VHS player in December of 1982, my first two store bought tapes were Abbott and Costello's "**Africa Screams**" and "**National Lampoon's Animal House**". Now, there's a broad range of comedy for you! And yes, I watched and freeze-framed the scene when John Belushi climbs the ladder to watch the sorority girls have a topless pillow fight while the stunning "Mandy Pepperidge" almost plays with herself.

During the next ten years or so, I watched a lot of movies in all genres. But in the teen comedy arena, "**Private School...for girls**" became a favorite as did "**My Tutor**", "**Hot Resort**", "**Hardbodies**", and "**Hot Dog...The Movie!**" (which is the only film I remember NOT being allowed to see in the theater due to my age.) So all these comedies and naked women made an impression on my young mind. At 14 years old, I had already decided to become a filmmaker and officially launched my professional career at the age of 20 with a now comedy/horror cult flick called, "**There's Nothing Out There**". It was a teen comedy, a monster movie, and a parody all rolled into one with nods to my comedy influences of "Abbott and Costello" and "**The Pink Panther**" movies, horror films like "**The Boogens**", "**Basket Case**", "**Friday The 13th**" horror/comedies like "**An American Werewolf In London**" and "**Fright Night**" and parodies like "**Student Bodies**", and Mel Brooks' films. It probably shouldn't have worked but it did and I was off and running. It really was a spoof but had enough nudity, violence, monsters, action, and smart stupidity to satisfy viewers over the last 30+ years.

As I was finishing post-production on the film in the beginning of 1990, I was also attending horror conventions to spread the word about my flick and met a fellow filmmaker named Jeff Burr who was promoting his directed "**Leatherface: Texas Chainsaw Massacre III**". He told me to look him up if I ever came out to Los Angeles. Well, six months later I was there and spent the day with Jeff. We had lunch and he took me to a special screening of Jim Wynorski's "**Nighty-Nightmare**" which was released later under the title "**Sorority House Massacre 2**". We then went to another friend of Jeff's, a screenwriter by the name of Kenneth J. Hall. Ken who was a special effects guy who also wrote and sometimes directed low-budget features. He had a shelf of produced screenplays with titles such as "**Evil Spawn**", "**Nightmare Sisters**", "**The Girl I Want**", "**Puppet Master**" and "**Dr. Alien**". I thought to myself, "I can do that" and when I got back to New York, as an exercise I started writing the first draft of "Hormones...The Movie!" In a way, it was almost an unofficial sequel to his script of "**Dr. Alien**".

So, that afternoon in L.A. was definitely an inspiration for me to write my first "teen sex comedy" or as I've later heard it called, "sci-awry comedy". Now what is a "Sci-Awry" comedy you may ask? Well, let me explain.

During the height of these teen "coming of age sex comedies", there was a sub-division to the genre where elements of science fiction, fantasy or just plain magic got involved with our horny guys looking for sex. In many cases, the most often used device was the all elusive "aphrodisiac" routine. Again, remember this was decades before Viagra came to be. An aphrodisiac was used to sexual arouse a women (usually) so she would be willing to have sex with any guy, even the losers who starred in these films! The hunt for the all powerful "Spanish Fly" appeared in films like in the Tom Cruise and Shelley Long flick, "**Losin' It**" and "**Screwballs**". In "**Porky's**", it took the form of the smell in the boy's locker room that turned Kim Cattrall from a shy teacher into a very loud nymphomaniac! Love potions were also a favorite in many of these films. It was an easy way to get the hot girl to suddenly want to get naked and have sex. Since these kind of immediate sexual stimulators don't really exist, an element of "science fiction" came into play. This very male-oriented fantasy made an impression on me in such films as "**Zapped!**", "**The Party Animal**", "**The Man Who Wasn't There**", "**The Invisible Kid**", "**Love Potion #9**", "**Weird Science**" "**Getting Lucky**" and the Chevy Chase starrer "**Modern Problems**" of which many gags were later borrowed for Jim Carrey's "**Liar Liar**".

In these films, the science fiction element became the major plot premise. A guy suddenly, due to drinking something or getting hit by radiation or finding a genie or making a deal with the devil or gaining telekinesis, would become irresistible to women. Or at the very least, use their new powers to see girls naked. In "**Zapped!**", Scott Baio uses his powers to undress most of his high school classmates including the amazing Heather Thomas, although a body double was used in the final film.

Steve Guttenberg becomes invisible and of course, journeys into the girl's college locker room before have sex (while still invisible) with the lovely Lisa Langlois. Sandra Bullock and Tate Donovan accidentally invent the ultimate aphrodisiac that affects their voices making all men or women attracted to them. In "**Modern Problems**" Chevy Chase gets sprayed with some nuclear waste that gives him the power to mentally give his girlfriend, Patti D'Arbanville a string of the best orgasms of her life! As I said, Jim Carrey later does the same thing to Jennifer Aniston in "**Liar Liar**" in the bathroom.

So, it is in this sub-division of teen comedies where "**Dr. Alien**" falls as well as does my first sci-awry comedy, "Hormones". I originally wrote this script in the summer of 1990. I really did it as an exercise to see if I could write one of these things. I had no story idea when I started so I wrote an opening sequence where about ten weird things happen before jumping back in time two days earlier. So my challenge was to figure out how to explain all those weird events in the next 90 pages and make this scene "logical" in the story. (NOTE: I do not recommend writing a script in this fashion. It is probably foolish and will be a mess.) But I did it and knocked off this script in five days. I thought it was silly but fun and hit many of the sci-awry teen sex comedy tropes. I had an aphrodisiac, I had aliens, I had invisibility, I had time travel, school bullies, the hot cheerleader, funny animals, and a sexual Armageddon! I decided to see if I could sell this crazy thing and I almost did, multiple times!

First I sent the script to David DeCoteau who had directed "**Dr. Alien**". I had seen many of DeCoteau's films growing up since he was very productive in the sexploitation field with such films as "**Sorority Babes In The Slimeball Bowl-A-Rama**". I probably got his contact info from Ken Hall. I figured if anyone would appreciate this script, David would. And guess what? He did! Took him a few weeks but after he read it, he called me and wanted to get together.

Luckily, I was heading back to California for another visit because my first film, **"There's Nothing Out There"** was going to have a special screening at Amblin Entertainment for Robert Zemeckis! But that's another story.

Well, as fate would have it, I met with DeCoteau in the morning to discuss "Hormones" a few hours before my screening of "Nothing" for Zemeckis. Both meetings/screenings went well but I didn't end up selling my script or start working for Amblin. DeCoteau definitely saw the influences of **"Dr. Alien"** and was interested but didn't find the funding to make it. Years later, I would actually write a lot of scripts for DeCoteau but funny enough, none of them were teen sex comedies.

So, years go by and I move out to Los Angeles and eventually run into another producer named Ted Chalmers. He liked my writing and loved "Hormones". He was good friends with actress Brinke Stevens at the time and attached her to the project to play the hot science teacher, Ms. Puddle. He also had a connection to Julie Strain, a larger than life (6'2") Penthouse model turned actress to play the lead Hormonious! Both were perfect for the roles. Ted decided to put together some artwork to help sell the movie and we did a one day photo shoot with Brinke, Julie, a friend of mine from college, Josh Seth and a few actresses he knew including Athena Massey, who went on to become a bit of a sexy superstar herself in movies like **"Poison Ivy 3"** with Jamie Pressly. So we threw together a one-sheet movie poster that I would have definitely rented if I was a 14 year old boy with a synopsis of the script on the back. We had an investor lined up in New York who was going to finance the project and started getting submissions from actors to audition. I thought we were going to make it this time but the money fell through days before we were going to start casting and production was off. I was annoyed, especially since this investor had wanted to make "Hormones" and a sequel! He wanted me to write a few scenes for Julie Strain for the sequel so I wound up writing the whole sequel script for free. I called it "Hormones 2: Raging Hormones". That didn't get made either.

So, time goes by. I make other movies but still didn't get my chance to do my teen comedy. I think the real reason "Hormones" had fallen apart is that these type of movies had fallen out of style at the time. In the mid-to late 90s, all teen comedies had turned into PG-13 flicks like **"Can't Hardly Wait"**, **"She's All That"**, and **"Never Been Kissed"**. Nudity was out and so were the "R" rated raunchy comedies.

As fate would have it, this all changed when **"American Pie"** hit the scene in 1999. Suddenly, it was proven the genre could be successful again and a few years later, another producer in Vegas, Michael Mahal, optioned my "Hormones" script to almost make it once again but it never came to be. By this point, I wasn't too heart-broken though because I finally did get to make my teen sexy comedy in 2000 called **"Pretty Cool"**. (NOTE: This script will be discussed at a later time in a later release, I believe.)

But let's backtrack a bit. In 1996 after I had officially moved to California, I met a French producer named Alain Siritzky who was famous for the softcore erotic entry called, "Emmanuelle". I got in the door with Siritzky's company by showing him my screenplay for "Hormones" and my flick **"Nothing Out There"**. He had just produced a series called **"Emmanuelle In Space"** starring Krista Allen and was about to make another bunch of late-night cable soft-erotic comedies for Cinemax and I became the go-to guy there for a while. These adventures will also be discussed later when my Siritzky screenplays are released so I won't go into all of these stories now either. Let's just say that many of my ideas for "Hormones" were incorporated into my **"Click"** and **"Butterscotch"** scripts and later into a series called **"Emmanuelle 2000"** which was produced on the heels of the success of **"American Pie"**. Siritzky wanted to make an "Emmanuelle Pie" high school sexy comedy. I agreed to do it since "Hormones" had never seen the light of day… until now.

So, in short, there's a little background history of the genre and my influences that led to this still unproduced screenplay of "Hormones". By now, I had pretty much given up that this script would ever be made so when Bare Manor Publishing approached me about publishing some of my sexy screenplays, I realized this was my chance to at least let people read what I tried to make back in 1990. And here we are. 2020 going on 2021. Thirty years since I first wrote this "epic". I do think I've improved as a writer over the years but there is a silly innocence to this script that I believe some might still enjoy. I was playing with the formula, trying to put my own spin on it, while throwing in everything including the kitchen sink!

So for those who miss the 80s sex comedies and always wished someone would have made a sequel to **"Dr. Alien"** or **"The Party Animal"** or **"Weird Science"** (amazingly none of these had sequels), here's one you probably would have enjoyed in say, 1984 if it had ever been produced into a feature film. And remember, if you like it, the sequel is already written and ready to go as well. Perhaps Bare Manor will release that screenplay soon too!

In conclusion, I was twenty-one years old when I wrote this script so don't judge me too harshly and please, read it with a sense of humor.

Best Regards,

Rolfe Kanefsky

HORMONES......The Movie!

FADE IN:

INT. BEDROOM - DAY.

SLOW MOTION C.U. of a baseball bat flying directly at the CAMERA. The bat hits, not the CAMERA, but a mirror that is in the room. The mirror shatters and the bat falls to the floor.

KEN ASHBROOK runs into the center of the room and spins around looking for something/someone. He is 18 years old, handsome but now very messy and extremely angry.

>   KEN
> Where are you?! Where the hell are
> you?!!

Ken catches a glimpse of something disappearing under the bed. Ken throws himself on to the floor and reaches under the bed for it.

>   KEN (CONT'D)
> Come on! Come on out of there, you
> slimy, little piece of concocted
> garbage...!

P.O.V. of something under bed as it dodges Ken's attempts to grab it, staying just out of reach of Ken's hand.

>   VOICE(from under bed)
> Now, I really think you're slightly
> overreacting...

>   KEN
> Overreacting?!! I'll show
> You overreacting!!....OW!!
>   (pulls hands away
>   from bed)
> You bit me! You asshole!!

Ken jumps up and pulls the bed away from the wall. As he does this, something quickly darts out from under the bed. It runs between Ken's legs and into the dark walk-in closet. Ken looks down to see it enter the closet. He grabs the bat and runs over to the closet.

>   KEN (CONT'D)
> You're really starting to piss me
> off now!!

Suddenly the door to Ken's bedroom bursts open! Two beautiful **WOMEN** in their early twenties wearing nothing but panties enter the room. Ken looks over at them.

                    KEN(fed up) (CONT'D)
          Oh, shit!

The two women run happily over to Ken. Ken quickly jumps
into the closet and slams the door behind him. The women run
over to the door and try to open it.

                                              CUT TO:

INT. CLOSET - DAY.

Ken locks the closet door. He can hear the women scratching
on the other side. Ken steps back from the door and turns on
a small overhanging light. The closet is very messy. Clothes
and toys cover the place. There is one window in the closet.

                    KEN(to what he was chasing)
          If you don't get me out of this one,
          I will make sure that your artificial
          life ends very horribly and painfully!

                    VOICE
                (from corner)
          Okay, okay. Go to the window. Open
          it.

Ken runs over to the window and looks out. He is on the second
floor. The backyard is down below. Ken throws the window
open.

Suddenly, there's a flash of light in the corner of the room.
Ken looks over to see a parrot wobble out of the corner.

Parrot P.O.V. as it flies past Ken, straight out the open
window and into the sky.

                    KEN
          Wait!! Come back here!! You son-of-
          a...! I'm gonna get you for this!!

Ken is trapped. He picks up a large toy to defend himself.
The women are almost through the door.

                                              CUT TO:

EXT. KEN'S HOUSE - BACKYARD - DAY.

A ladder lays in the corner of the yard. Two female hands
reach down and pick it up.

                                              CUT TO:

INT. KEN'S HOUSE - CLOSET - DAY.

Ken takes his stance with the toy. He swings it back, ready
to strike. Ken hears something bang against the house. Ken
looks out the window and sees the ladder.

                    FEMALE VOICE
             I'll meet you at the lab!

Ken looks upset but quickly climbs out the window.

He is halfway out when the closet door gives way and the two women run in.

                    NAKED WOMAN 1
             Kenny!! Don't go!!

                    NAKED WOMAN 2
             Come back!! Kenny!!!

They run over to the window and try to grab him.

                                                  CUT TO:

EXT. HOUSE - DAY.

Ken is climbing down the ladder. The women's hands reach out and grab parts of his shirt. Ken struggles to break loose and climb down. His shirt is pulled off as he continues down the ladder. The women scream after him.

Ken, without shirt, jumps down the last few rungs and runs around the house. He darts out into the road just as a car comes speeding by. Ken, without shirt, freezes in the middle of the street and looks at the approaching car!

                                                  CUT TO:

INT. CAR - DAY.

KEN ASHBROOK is behind the wheel. He is looking down at the tape deck. He is 18 years old, attractive but dressed as a nerd and looks very proper. He glances up from the tape deck and catches a glimpse of shirtless Ken Ashbrook standing in the middle of the road. Shirtless Ken suddenly vanishes! Ken drives right past where Ken was standing.

Ken looks back to see nobody. He shrugs and continues to drive down the road. He inserts a tape and MUSIC begins as a subtitle fades in that read:

"**ONE DAY EARLIER---** (Don't worry, you'll understand soon.)"

Ken's car continues down the road.

                                                  CUT TO:

EXT. HIGH SCHOOL - MORNING.

OPENING CREDITS START

It is your typical public high school and the location of summer school for a few classes of unhappy students. Some students are arriving. The music from the tape deck continues to play during this arrival at school MONTAGE.

A car drives by the high school with a bunch of kids who don't have to attend classes this summer.

                    KID IN CAR(yelling)
          SUCKERS!!!

The car drives by as Ken's car pulls into the school's parking lot. Ken gets out of his car. He looks at his watch which reads 7:35. He opens up the trunk and pulls out a cardboard box. Ken heads for the school with the cardboard box in his hands.

A group of B.A.B.E.S. (Beautiful and bitchy, extremely stupid) high school girls gather around Ken and follow him.

JENNY CASHMAN is the leader of the group. She is a true B.A.B.E. She walks in front of Ken, teasing as she talks. The other four circle Ken.

                    JENNY
          I've got a message for you from Dan.

                    KEN
               (trying to ignore
                them)
          Tell him that there's nothing to
          worry about. I've got his experiment
          right here.

                    JENNY
          He says that you better have his
          experiment with you and working.

                    KEN
          Ah, well good. Thanks for relaying
          that. Tell him everything's under
          control.

                    JENNY
          He wants to know what your answer
          is.

                    KEN
               (thinking for a second)
          You memorized his message, didn't
          you?... Okay, tell him the answer is
          everything is here and working. Would
          you like me to write that down for
          you?

                    JENNY
          I'll tell him. Oh, and he better get
          an A for your sake.

KEN
I'll mention that to Ms. Puddle. I'm just the teacher's aid, remember?

JENNY
(turning away)
Let's go, girls.

The four girls follow. They head back to a group of **M.A.C.H.O.S.** (mean, annoying, cheating, handsome, obnoxious, stuck-up) jocks.

KEN(as the girls leave)
Bye Cindy, Mindy, Candy, Becky. Nice talking to you.

The four girls look back slightly confused, shrug and continue on. Ken watches them go.

MARTIN TURKEL joins Ken. He is Ken's 17 year old, comical best friend. He looks where Ken is looking.

MARTIN
Nothing like beginning the day with a friendly threat from the boobie bunch.

KEN(looking over)
Hi, Martin.

MARTIN
Did you do Dan the man's science project for him?

KEN
Yep.

MARTIN
Did you ask any girls out? No. Did you study all night? Yes. Do you ever have fun? No. Are you familiar with the word nerd? Yes...

KEN
I'm not a nerd.

MARTIN
Ken, this is summer school. I'm here because I have to be. You volunteered. I think that about sums it up.

KEN
Extra credit never hurts and I couldn't leave you here to suffer alone.

                    MARTIN
          Oh, I hate to be the one that cuts
          into your precious time with Kelly
          Brown. The other..."social wonder".

                    KEN
          Kelly Brown and I are science people.

                    MARTIN
          Does that mean you two have wild
          nights of sex together?

                    KEN(entering school)
          No, we don't. Kelly is just my
          assistant and she _is_ a nerd.

                    MARTIN(entering)
          I have trouble seeing the difference.

                                             CUT TO:

INT. BASEMENT LAB - MORNING.

This basement has been converted into a laboratory. There
are vials, bubbling liquids, little machines that beep, little
machines that flash lights. There is a cage of gerbils, a
cage of mice, and a fish tank.

There are a couple of multicolored glass bottles in the
foreground with special labels on them and a fairly large
satellite dish that is aimed up and out the small basement
window to the sky.

There is a computer connected to the dish. A large telescope
is next to the computer and is also pointed up at the window.

Suddenly the door to the basement opens.

KELLY BROWN enters. She is 18 years old and very bookish.
She wears the ugliest of glasses and clothes. Of course, she
is attractive underneath but who could tell. She is dressed
for school and is also a very neat person.

Kelly walks over to the special bottles and opens up a
notebook of notes. She takes out a small tape recorder and
presses record.

                    KELLY(into tape recorder)
          July 15. 7:45 a.m. After a grueling
          night of scientific study with Ken
          Ashbrook and having to deal with my
          older sister and her two European
          pen pals who are still crashing in
          our living room, I have finally come
          up with what may just be the key to
          the entire experiment.
                    (MORE)

                    KELLY(into tape recorder) (CONT'D)
              (glancing over at the
               dish and computer
               which has a blank
               screen)
          Still no contact has been made with
          the alternate universe that I
          discovered last week...
              (looks through
               telescope)
          But I know that will require a bit
          more time. Anyway, Project Hormonious
          is almost solved. I can feel it in
          my bones.

Kelly moves back to the multicolored bottles. She pulls out
a large bowl and a couple of other powder chemicals.

                    KELLY(into recorder) (CONT'D)
          I've decided that the separate
          mixtures are all on the right track
          but they must be combined to reach
          the productive results. That plus
          the chemical BLTX2, to give it a
          little punch, should be very
          interesting to watch....Here it
          goes....

Kelly unplugs each of the bottles. Some stream rises from
the open tops. She then slowly and carefully pours some of
the three bottles into the bowl. A few sparks shoot out of
the swirling liquid.

                                                    CUT TO:

INT. SCHOOL HALLWAY - MORNING.

Ken and Martin enter, talking. Other students pass by.

                    KEN
          Martin, I know my lifestyle might
          not seem that exciting to you but
          when you're trying to change the
          course of mankind...

                    MARTIN
          Did it ever occur to you that mankind
          doesn't want its course changed?

                    KEN
              (entering classroom)
          Of course they do. They just don't
          know it because they're too busy...

                    MARTIN
               (entering classroom)
          Having a good time? Ken, baby.
          Hormones make the world run. You
          can't just put an end to them.

                                             CUT TO:

INT. BASEMENT LAB - DAY.

Kelly finishes pouring the liquids together. The liquids
start to bubble. Kelly looks at weird mixture slightly
confused. She then takes the powder and pours it in. A loud
sizzling sound starts to rise from the chemicals. It is
building up. Kelly is completely baffled by this.

                    KELLY
          I have combined the mixtures but I'm
          not sure why it's sizzling and
          bubbling.

The sound continues to build. Smoke starts to rise from the
bowl. Kelly suddenly realizes and looks down. She accidentally
placed the bowl on top of a portable burner and it's on!

Kelly reaches to pull the bowl off but it is too hot. She
pulls her hands away and drops the tape recorder. The sound
is building to what can only be one thing.

                    KELLY (CONT'D)
          Oh Shit!!

Kelly runs as fast as she can to the door. CAMERA moves in
on the sizzling and bubbling multicolored liquids. The animals
in the cages are running around and around.

Sure enough, there is an explosion!

                                             CUT TO:

INT. EMPTY SCIENCE CLASSROOM - DAY.

Ken and Martin enter. Ken puts the box down on a desk.

                    KEN
          I'm not trying to destroy hormones.
          I'm trying to control them. Do you
          know how much more we could accomplish
          if we could control our hormones?
          Especially during our early adolescent
          years.

                    MARTIN
          Yeah, yeah. Not to mention all the
          money saved on pimple cream. Look,
          Kenny.
                         (MORE)

8.

MARTIN (CONT'D)
Puberty and sexual awakening is an important stage of human life. And sex is fun. A lot of people are having a great deal of fun with that topic right now and you could be one of them...provided you could find a willing partner. But I've seen these ads...

KEN
If I wanted to find a girlfriend, I could do so without the use of a down-payment, thank you very much.

MARTIN
Then take the plunge. Why try to ruin everybody's good time?

KEN
I am not ruining a good time. Do you know how many people are also miserable because of their hormones and sex drive?

MARTIN
I can think of one.

KEN
Very funny. I'm just trying to invent a way for people to control themselves. Just think how a formula like this would help the problem of self-abuse in this world. Sexual distractions could be replaced by analytical research.

MARTIN
Wild parties could be replaced by board room meetings.

KEN
Exactly!

MARTIN
I love the sound of it. Ken, if I thought you had anyway of inventing a formula like this, you do know that I'd shoot you dead right now.

KEN
Just wait, Martin. You'll see how much clearer your thoughts are. No more day dreams of half naked women. No more money wasted on issues of porno magazines or video tapes.

                    MARTIN
You're really making me mad now. Why
don't you just hurry up and get laid
already!? Then you can really start
to do something constructive with
your time.

                    KEN
          (unpacking the box)
We'll see. We'll see.

                    MARTIN
          (thinking to himself)
I could probably hire someone to
come over to your house. A real
professional...

                    KEN:
Don't you dare.

                    MARTIN:
Huge breasts, long legs, strong
thighs...

                    KEN
Cut it out.

                    MARTIN
Tie you down. Strip naked. Teach you
the meaning of a good time.

                    DAN
          (from doorway)
Discussing tonights homo activities,
I see!!

Ken and Martin spin around to see **DAN**, an 18 year old, tough, bully jock and leader of the group of five M.A.C.H.O.S. that stand in the doorway. They enter.

                    MARTIN(playing with it)
Oh, Ken. We've been discovered and
by the intellectual group too. How
you doing Dan, Biff, Bart, Brad,
Eugene?

                    EUGENE
That's Gino!

                    MARTIN
          (acting gay)
Sorry, Gino. Any of you boys want to
play?

                    BIFF
Get the fuck away from me, fairy!

                    MARTIN
               (strolling out of the
                room)
          Well, if you change your mind, I'll
          be in Home Economics. Toodles.

Martin waltzes out of the room, leaving Ken alone with the "men".

                    GINO
          I didn't know they had a summer school
          class for home economics?

Dan just shoots Gino a look. He turns to Ken.

                    DAN(to Ken)
          Did you get my message from Jenny?

                    KEN
          I got it.

                    DAN
          Well?

                    KEN
               (unsure what he wants)
          Well, she gives good message.

                    DAN
          No. How's my project?! She couldn't
          remember your answer.

                    KEN
               (lifting something
                out of box)
          Oh. Here you go.

                    DAN
               (looking at it)
          What is it?

                    KEN
          It's an auto-jog heat reducer.

                    DAN
          A what?

                                                  CUT TO:

INT. SCIENCE CLASS - LATER MORNING.

Every student is around their special creation. The teacher, **MS. PUDDLE**, a bookish, timid, intelligent female in her early thirties is speaking to Dan who is holding up his project.

                          DAN(a little nervous) (CONT'D)
                    Ah,...a auto heat jog...No, a auto-
                    jog heat reducer. Um, he ah, I mean,
                    I'll show you how it works.

A couple of the other students giggle as Dan puts on the
device. The machine is a big belt with a weird black box on
the front of it. Dan ties it around his waist.

                          DAN (CONT'D)
                    You see, you strap it on and adjust
                    the fan thing...
                         (tilts the black fan
                          box up towards his
                          face)
                    ...And then when you jog or exercise
                    you just press this button and...

Dan turns it on and suddenly a burst of cool air starts to
blow out from the box. The air blows straight at his face
and causes his air to fly up. He looks pretty stupid. The
other students laugh.

                          DAN (CONT'D)
                    So when you jog, it...keeps...
                    you...cool... What's so funny?

                          MS. PUDDLE
                    Nothing, nothing. It's very good,
                    Dan. I'm just amazed that someone
                    who usually puts his looks above
                    everything else would create something
                    that is...more useful than attractive.

                          DAN
                    What do you mean?

Dan glances at a mirror and starts to freak out.

                          DAN (CONT'D)
                    Why that son-of-a....!!!

Ken starts to drift towards the door. Dan presses the other
buttons to turn it off. He presses reverse and "high" speed.
Dan's hair immediately flies down in his face. His shirt
then rips off and flies into the machine! Dan tilts the box
away from him.

Ms. Puddle, who is wearing a tight long skirt, is still
standing in front of him. Suddenly her skirt is ripped off
and flies into the machine! She screams and tries to cover
herself. She runs forward and attempts yanking her skirt out
of the machine.

The machine is tilted up slightly as they struggle. It
continues to suck and Ms. Puddle's blouse is suddenly rip
off and eaten by the machine!

Ken closes the door behind him as the chaos builds in the room.

CUT TO:

INT. SCHOOL BATHROOM - DAY.

Ken is pacing back and forth. Martin is peeking out the door for any sign of Dan.

                  MARTIN
The word is you're dead, you know.

                  KEN
I know. I know. Look, did I ask him to press reverse?

                  MARTIN
Doesn't matter.

                  KEN
I know. We're dealing with humanoids without brains.

                  MARTIN
Listen, it's almost lunch time. If you can get out of here, just don't come back. Your parents are away for the week, right? Don't answer the phone. Don't answer the door. Don't leave your house.

                  KEN
Thanks a lot.

                  MARTIN
But seriously, Ken. No matter what happens. I want you to know that I'm proud of you. My best friend invented an instant clothing remover. Years of scientific study have finally paid off. I think this can qualify you as a candidate for the Nobel Prize.

Suddenly the bathroom door bursts open. Ken jumps into one of the stalls and locks it. Kelly enters. She doesn't look so clean anymore. She's covered with smoke, hair sticking up, etc...

                  MARTIN (CONT'D)
Don't worry. It's just Kelly. Kelly?!! What are you doing here? This is the boys bathroom.

                    KEN
              (coming out of stall)
          Oh my God. What happened?

                    KELLY (long pause)
          I made a mistake.

                    KEN
          You made a mistake.

                    DAN
          No! You made a mistake, pal!

Dan and his gang are standing in the doorway. Dan is wearing
another shirt but his hair still gives away what happened.

Dan pushes Kelly to the side and moves forward. They do a
double-take at each other for a moment.

                    KEN
          Now, Dan. Lets try to calmly put
          this situation into perspective.

                    DAN
          I'm going to put your face into
          perspective.

                    KELLY
              (softly to Martin)
          Did I miss something?

                    MARTIN
              (nodding)
          Yeah. Another mistake. More serious.

                    KEN
              (backing up)
          Dan. This machine works but you have
          to be running. Then the hair doesn't,
          ah...

                    DAN
              (making a fist)
          Running, huh?

Suddenly the bell rings. The others turn.

                    KEN
          Yeah, running.

Dan swings at him. Ken pulls open the door stall in front of
his face. Dan's fist slams into the metal door. He pulls
back in pain. Ken makes a break for it. He runs past the
others, distracted by the bell.

                    MARTIN
          And they're off!!!

Dan and his group run out of the bathroom after Ken. MUSIC comes up at this point.

CUT TO:

INT. SCHOOL HALLWAYS - DAY.

The chase is on! Ken flies down the hallway. Dan and the others are close behind. Ken turns a corner to see a ladder right in front of him. There is a girl hanging a sign from the top of the ladder. Ken has no way to turn.

He falls to his knees and slides across the tile floor and through the opening in the ladder. Ken looks up as he slides by to catch a quick look under the girl's skirt. He jumps to his feet again and continues to run.

Dan and the others aren't so graceful. The ladder and the girl come crashing to the floor. The girl actually lands right on top of Dan's head. Her legs wrap around his back and his head disappears under her skirt. The girl screams. Dan falls to the ground and the girl jumps off.

CUT TO:

INT. BASEMENT LAB - DAY.

The place is a mess. Slimy liquid is dripping from everything. Liquid is pouring out of the bowl and flowing onto the floor. The dish is covered with the stuff.

CAMERA shifts to the computer, which has some of the stuff on it. Strange symbols and backward numbers and letters fill the screen.

CUT TO:

INT. GYM - MEN'S LOCKER ROOM - DAY.

Ken, looking for an exit, enters the locker room. He runs around rows of lockers as Dan and the others come crashing in.

Ken pulls over a rack of sports balls. Balls bounce everywhere. Ken runs through the showers and throws every bar of soap that's sitting on soap dishes to the floor.

Dan and his gang manage to make it through the balls. Some slip on the soap. Dan takes a tumble.

Ken tears out of the locker room. Dan's gang, minus Dan, follow.

Dan pulls himself up and is about to follow when a **BIG GYM TEACHER** stops him. Dan stumbles back, nervously.

The gym teacher, a large german man in very good shape and wearing an outfit that shows it off, stands in Dan's way. He is not happy.

>   GYM TEACHER(with accent)
>   What are you doing here? In my locker
>   room?
>
>   DAN
>   I...I was just leaving.
>
>   GYM TEACHER
>   (seeing soap)
>   You knock over my soap?! You pick up
>   my soap now!
>   (Dan hesitates)
>   Bend down and pick up the soap! You
>   do what I say, ya'? OR ELSE!!

Dan slowly bends down. He is scared shitless. He picks up one of the bars of soap and hands it to the gym teacher.

>   GYM TEACHER (CONT'D)
>   That's good. You drop something. You
>   pick it up. You remember that.
>
>   DAN
>   Am I in trouble or...can I go?
>
>   GYM TEACHER
>   (after a long look)
>   I pardon you.

Dan hesitates for a second and then slowly slips by the gym teacher. He runs out of the locker rooms.

                                                       CUT TO:

INT. BASEMENT LAB - DAY.

The bowl is still bubbling over. The dish starts to move by itself.

It adjusts itself and points a little higher out the window. More symbols and weird letters appear on the computer screen. A red laser suddenly shoots from the sky, through the basement window, and into the dish. The entire dish starts to glow red!

                                                       CUT TO:

EXT. SCHOOL - DAY.

Ken bursts out the door and into the parking lot. He heads for his car when Jenny and her group jump out from behind it.

                          JENNY
                There he is!! Get him!!

Jenny and the others run towards Ken. Ken sees what's coming.

                          KELLY(O.S.)
                Ken! Over here!!

Ken turns. He sees Kelly waving by her car. He runs for it.
Jenny and the girls chase them through the parked cars. Dan
and his group suddenly burst into the lot and run right in
front of the girls. Both groups collide into each other.
Boys and girls go flying. They all wind up in a big pile on
the ground.

Ken and Kelly leap into Kelly's car. She turns the key, steps
on the gas, and the car roars out of the school grounds!

                                                    CUT TO

INT. KELLY'S CAR - DAY.

Ken looks back to see the school disappear behind them.

                     KELLY(smiling) (CONT'D)
                I did pretty good, huh?

                          KEN
                   (turns back to Kelly,
                    not smiling)
                You made a mistake?...What mistake?

Kelly quickly loses her smile.

                                                    CUT TO:

EXT. KELLY'S HOUSE - DAY.

Kelly's car pulls up in front of the house. Yelling can be
heard inside the car.

                     KEN(from car) (CONT'D)
                That's a mistake?!! No, that's not a
                mistake!!! That's a MAJOR FUCK-UP!!!

Ken gets out of car. Kelly follows slowly behind.

                          KEN (CONT'D)
                I don't believe you!! ONE YEAR!! One
                full year I've been working on this
                and one night you get a sudden urge
                to just... just COMBINE THE FORMULAS!
                     (walking towards house)
                Oh, I can't wait to see this.
                     (turns away)

17.

>   No, I don't want to see it. I don't
>   want to see it!! I want to kill you
>   instead.
>   (turning back to house)
>   No, I'll see it first. Then I'll
>   kill you. It will give me more
>   motivations!!
>   (turning back again)
>   How could you do this to me?!! All
>   I wanted to do was invent something
>   to help mankind and
>   you...EXPERIMENT!!!
>   (turning back to house)
>   Oh, let me at it! Lets see my year
>   of hard labor!!!

Ken enters the house. Kelly follows behind.

>   CUT TO:

INT. BASEMENT LAB - DAY.

Ken bursts into the basement. The liquid is still flowing and is now ankle deep. Ken barges right in, steps into the liquid, and slips in a big way. He flips backwards in a complete arc and lands face and body flat down in the liquid with a big splash!

Everything has settled by the time Kelly reaches the basement. She stands in the doorway, just out of the liquid.

Ken pulls his head out of the liquid. He is covered with a jello-like slime. He looks back at Kelly and then looks at the room and what he's in.

>   KEN (CONT'D)
>   This is good. This is really good.
>   Much better than I could have even
>   imagined...Um, this stuff I'm laying
>   in...It isn't toxic or anything? Not
>   that I really care anymore. It's
>   just that I still have the curiosity
>   of a scientist even though
>   I'm NEVER GOING TO BECOME ONE!!!!
>
>   VOICE:
>   (from dark corner of
>   room)
>   Hi.

Ken and Kelly turn to the voice.

>   KELLY
>   Who's there? Who are you?

The person in the corner walks into the light. She is a beautiful, perfectly proportioned **20-something year old WOMAN** wearing only a very skimpy bikini. She is standing in the liquid.

                    PERFECT WOMAN
          Well, I don't know how to explain
          exactly but I'm Hormonious, your sex
          drive.

                    KEN
               (starting to get up)
          Aha. That's exactly what I thought.
          Okay, Kelly. This is fun. You and
          Martin teamed up and bought me a
          prostitute. Thank-you ever so much.

                    KELLY
               (confused)
          Hormonious? But that's the name of
          our....

                    HORMONIOUS
          ...experiment. I know. You succeeded.
          I'm here.

                    KEN
               (sloshing through the
                liquid)
          And April first was three months
          ago. I'm not going to play this,
          okay? You're a hooker...
               (turns to Kelly)
          You destroyed the experiment, and
          I'm standing in a puddle of goop
          which used to have some scientific
          purpose. So Kelly, pay her. You can
          then just leave because I am in
          absolutely no mood for sex right
          now.

                    HORMONIOUS
          That's going to be a problem.

                    KEN
          Not my problem. Talk to Kelly. I'm
          taking a shower.

                    HORMONIOUS
          It won't do any good. It's already
          too late.

                    KEN
          Pardon me?

                    HORMONIOUS
          Let me try to explain. You see I'm
          not really a girl...I'm your...sex
          drive.

KEN
That's some ego you got, isn't it?

HORMONIOUS
What I mean is not just your sex drive... I'm everyone and everything's sex drive... made living, I think.

KEN
(turns to Kelly)
Did you write this?

Kelly shakes her head. She is just as confused as Ken.

KEN(back to Hormonious) (CONT'D)
Listen, a sex drive is part of a person or animal. It's part of the brain. It is not a full force by itself.

HORMONIOUS
Is now. In fact, you're standing in me.

KEN
(looks down at goop)
No, no, sorry. Don't buy it. A person can't form from goop. It has to become a bug, then an insect, then an animal...

HORMONIOUS
Well, I can be all those things.

She hops up on one of the counter and in a flash changes into a fly, then a mouse, then a turtle, then a rabbit, then a dog, then a monkey, and then a male bodybuilder who is only wearing a skimpy bathing suit.

MAN HORMONIOUS
See. I can become anything that has a sex drive.

KEN
Because that's what you are.

HORMONIOUS
Right.

KEN
So, why are you a male bodybuilder now?

HORMONIOUS
Because I took the shape of your fantasy.

                    KEN
          Bullshit!!

                    HORMONIOUS
          No, I meant her fantasy. I was yours
          before.

Ken and Kelly look at each other for a beat. Ken turns back.

                    KEN(very calmly)
          Okay, I see. We just invented a shape-
          Shifting sex drive. Well, it all
          makes sense now.

                    HORMONIOUS
          Well, actually you invented a gooey
          sex drive. They invented the shape-
          shifting idea.

                    KEN
          They?

Hormonious points out the window. Ken runs over to the window.
Kelly starts to move.

                    HORMONIOUS(to Kelly)
          I wouldn't come in here if I were
          you.

Kelly pauses before stepping into the slime. She doesn't
understand but doesn't enter the room. Ken looks out the
window. He turns back to Kelly.

                    KELLY
          What is it?

                    KEN(calm)
          Oh, nothing. Just a spaceship that's
          crashed into your backyard.

                    KELLY
          A what?!!

                    KEN
            (walking away from
             window)
          It's very simple. You want to know
          what's happening? I understand. You
          see when I ran in here and slipped,
          I smashed my head against the floor.
          This is just a dream. You see? So,
          don't panic Kelly. You're just a
          part of my dream. Martin was right.
          I should get out more often.

                    KELLY
          Are you sure?

21.

                    KEN
          Try to scientifically explain this
          some other way. So, Hormonious, where
          are the aliens?

Hormonious points behind the basement door. Suddenly, a
glowing red light moves out from behind the door. It floats
in the air and stops in the center of the room.

                    KEN (CONT'D)
          Oh, right. Sorry, guys. I almost
          didn't recognize you.
               (laughing to himself)
          My mind is so warped.

                    FLOATING LIGHT
          This is not a dream.

                    KEN
          Says you. Look, Mr. Hormone. I just
          love talking to a part of my anatomy
          and everything. It's just that these
          floating guys are ruining what could
          be a really revealing conversation.
          Especially if you are Kelly's fantasy.
          I got some questions to ask you.

                    KELLY
          Don't you dare!

                    HORMONIOUS
          Ken, I'm not the one in control
          here...

                    KEN
          I know. I am. Turn back into the
          girl.

                    HORMONIOUS
          Okay.

Body builder suddenly turns back into the perfect girl in
the bikini seen earlier.

                    HORMONIOUS (CONT'D)
          What I was trying to say is that I'm
          not the only experiment that worked
          today. The power of my sex rays
          affected that radar thing...

                    KELLY
          My alternate universe. I reached
          you!!!

The glowing red light turns around to face Kelly who backs
up.

FLOATING LIGHT
So, you called us here.

KELLY (slyly)
How you doing?

KEN
Wait. You're saying she accidentally invented a material sex drive which in turn accidentally brought in aliens from another dimension into town.

KELLY (correcting)
Alternative universe.

KEN
Yeah, right. And these floating light balls made you flesh?...Oh man, do I need to seek some psychological help.

FLOATING LIGHT
We wanted to know how a planet that is so underdeveloped could contact us when it isn't supposed to happen for another 200 years. We made your chemical human to explain what it is composed of.

KEN
That's a nice talent you have. What else can you do?

FLOATING LIGHT
We can do anything. So we gave Hormonious some of our powers to match its substance.

HORMONIOUS
That's right. They can do anything except take off again.

KELLY
Bummer.

KEN
Oh yeah? Why's that?

FLOATING LIGHT
Our ship was pulled too quickly into your ozone field. We cannot repair the ship.

KELLY
Ever?

                        FLOATING LIGHT
                Not until your planet invents the
                right materials which don't exist
                yet here.

                        KEN
                    (to himself)
                I've got to write this one down when
                I wake up.

                        KELLY'S MOTHER (O.S.)
                    (from upstairs)
                I'm back from shopping!! Anyone home?

                        KELLY
                    (spinning around)
                Oh, shit. My mother! What are we
                going to do?!

                        FLOATING LIGHT
                About what?

                        KELLY
                About everything. You, Hormonious,
                your ship, this mess!!!

                        KEN
                Kelly, you can't get in trouble in a
                dream.

                        FLOATING LIGHT
                    (looking around)
                Oh, don't worry.

                        KELLY'S MOTHER
                    (coming down stairs)
                Kelly, are you in the basement again?

Suddenly the floating light expands and everything whites
out for a second. When the light disappears, everything is
back to normal.

The floating light, Hormonious, the spaceship outside the
window and the ankle-high slime has all disappeared. The
slime has been completely cleaned off everything and only a
bubbling bowl of it remains.

Ken, however, is still covered with the stuff. Kelly's mother
reaches the bottom of the basement stairs and looks in.

                        KELLY'S MOTHER (CONT'D)
                You are here. Oh, hello, Ken.
                Experimenting again?

Ken looks down and sees himself dripping.

                        KELLY
          Yes, mom.

                        KELLY'S MOTHER
                  (looking strangely at
                   them)
          Well, enjoy yourselves, I guess.
          Bye.

                        KEN
          Bye, Mrs. Brown.

She leaves. Kelly turns back to Ken.

                        KELLY
          Are you still dreaming or what?

                        KEN
          I don't know but I'm going to walk
          back to my house now. Why don't you
          call me up tomorrow or I'll call you
          tomorrow. Maybe I'll just sleep
          through tomorrow. Yeah, that sounds
          like a good idea. Bye.

Ken waddles out of the basement, leaving Kelly looking around confused.

                                        CUT TO:

EXT. SIDEWALK - DAY.

Ken, still covered with slime, slowly walks home trying to piece together everything that has happened, beginning with almost running himself over earlier. ROCK SONG: "Deep Love" comes up.

Ken passes some other houses on his way. He passes a man mowing his lawn. The man looks at Ken strangely. Ken nods and walks by.

He then passes a wooden fence. On the other side are two teen-age girls laying out in the sun by their pool. The girls sit up and smell the air as Ken passes.

A young woman rides by Ken on her bicycle. Ken keeps his head down to avoid the strange looks. The woman rides past and smells the air. She stops the bicycle short and looks back at Ken as he walks along. A look of excitement comes over her face. She readjusts herself on the bicycle seat.

Ken crosses past an intersection. Women in the stores run to the window and watch him pass. The men just look at him like he's crazy. The women are smiling and excited. Ken, who is embarrassed enough, walks faster.

A car with three **16 year old girls** drives by. They suddenly make a U-Turn and start following Ken. They drive up next to him and slow down to watch him. They are all excited. Ken looks over at them. The girls are smiling and bouncing up and down in their seats.

          KEN:
What's the matter? Haven't you ever seen a person covered with Hormonious before?

Ken turns away and quickly walks up his driveway and enters his house. The girls in the car squirm in their seats as they watch him go. They finally drive off.

          CUT TO:

INT. KEN'S BATHROOM - DAY.

Ken peels off the slime-drenched clothes and hops into the shower. He turns on the water and starts to wash. The jello-like slime does come off and washes away. He takes a sigh of relief as the slime washes away.

          KEN
Won't do any good. Yeah, right.

          HORMONIOUS
       (outside shower curtain)
But it won't.

          KEN
Who's there?

Suddenly the curtain is drawn slightly open and Hormonious in perfect girl figure with bikini enters the shower.

          KEN(trying to cover himself) (CONT'D)
Oh my God!

          HORMONIOUS
Nice to see you too.

          KEN
How'd you get in here?

          HORMONIOUS
Came through the cat door.

          KEN
As a cat, right?

          HORMONIOUS
You got it. What's wrong? You seem a little tense.

                    KEN
Well, I don't know why. I mean, I'm
just standing here naked with a girl
in a bikini in my shower.

                    HORMONIOUS
Oh, the bikini's bothering you.
          (she snaps her finger
           and in a flash, she
           completely naked)
Better?

                    KEN
Well, I guess in a way. That's, ah,
another trick the space light taught
you?

                    HORMONIOUS
Uh-huh. So, did you get a load of
what was happening out there?

                    KEN
Yeah, everyone was looking at me
like I was an asshole. But now I'm
all clean and everything's back to
normal if you would just disappear.

                    HORMONIOUS
Believe me, everything is not back
to normal. You didn't notice what
was happening outside?

                    KEN
People were staring at me because I
was covered with slime.

                    HORMONIOUS
The men were looking at you because
you were covered slime. And I don't
like being called slime, by the way.
The women had something else on their
minds.

                    KEN
          (grabbing a towel and
           exiting shower)
I don't believe this. Excuse me.

                    HORMONIOUS
          (following him out)
Listen, the shower doesn't do any
good. I absorb into you. You can't
get rid of me no matter what.

                    KEN
Oh yeah? Watch!

Ken leaves the bathroom and slams the door behind him.

CUT TO:

INT. KEN'S BEDROOM - DAY.

Ken enters after slamming the door to find Martin sitting in a chair, watching television. Ken freezes with the towel wrapped around his waist. Martin looks at him strangely.

                KEN (CONT'D)
Martin?!

                MARTIN
Hey. How you doing there, buddy? You, ah... talking to someone in the bathroom?

                KEN
No, um...I was just talking, you know. What are you doing here?

                MARTIN
Well, I wanted to be the first to congratulate you on that incredible escape from school today. Where'd you go after? Kelly's?

                KEN
Ah, yeah. Um, Martin, I've had a really strange day today.

                MARTIN
Besides Dan and the undressing machine?

                KEN
Uh-huh....Oh, hell with it!
        (walks over to closed
         bathroom door)
I want you to meet someone. I didn't think she was real but she's been bugging me all day and I don't know what to do about it...

                MARTIN
     (getting excited)
A girl?

               KEN
Brace yourself. She's crazy but definitely a knockout. Martin, meet Hormonious.

Ken swings open the bathroom door. The perfect girl is gone. Hormonious the cat slowly walks out of the bathroom, purring.

The cat rubs its head on Ken's leg. Ken and Martin look at the cat.

                    MARTIN
          You're right, Ken. She is some
          knockout.

Just look at that tail.

                    KEN (grabbing cat)
          No! Change back! Change back to that
          beautiful woman figure.

Ken shakes the cat around. Martin gets up.

                    MARTIN:
          Ah, Ken, I think we really have to
          find you a girl soon.

                    KEN
             (holding cat)
          No, you don't understand. This cat
          was a woman. But then she turned
          into a male body builder. She can do
          that sort of thing.

She said that the women on the street were looking at me strangely.

                    MARTIN
          Well, I don't know how to break this
          to you. But they usually look at you
          strangely.

                    KEN
          Yes, but Hormonious hinted that they
          all wanted to have sex with me!!

                    MARTIN
          The cat told you that women want to
          have sex with you. Well, Ken, I don't
          know. When cats start to tell me
          things, I don't always believe them.
          I mean, how do you know you can really
          trust your cat?

                    KEN
          This is not my cat!

                    MARTIN
          Oh, well then. What more can I say?

                    KEN
               (to cat)
          You hear that? Martin says that I
          shouldn't trust you. Martin's my
          best friend and I don't even know
          who you are. I don't want to see you
          again. I want you to stay out of my
          life and don't start bugging Kelly
          either. You hear me?!

                    MARTIN
          I think she heard you, Ken.

                    KEN
               (dropping cat and
                kicking it)
          Now get out of here and don't come
          back!!

The cat runs out of the room.

                    MARTIN
          That's the way to do it, Ken. Got to
          show those cats who they're dealing
          with sometimes. You let them start
          giving you advice and the next thing
          you know, they walk all over you.
          Especially during the night when
          you're trying to get some sleep.
          I know. I have two of them.

                    KEN
               (starting to think)
          I just yelled at a cat, didn't I?

                    MARTIN
          Yes you did, Ken.

                    KEN
               (turning and walking
                into closet)
          I'm losing my mind.

                    MARTIN
               (looking around
                bathroom)
          Could be. But I've suspected mental
          problems with you for a long time.

                    KEN
               (from closet)
          Thanks, Martin. I knew I could always
          count on you for support.

                    MARTIN
          Hey!
                    (MORE)

30.

                    MARTIN (CONT'D)
          I've warned you. No sex drive can be
          just as damaging as an overactive
          one.

                                                    CUT TO:

INT. BASEMENT LAB - DUSK.

Kelly is staring into the animal cages. She sees the mice
and the gerbils fucking like crazy. The cages are shaking
back and forth.

                    KELLY(to herself)
          This is very interesting.
               (picks up tape recorder
                and speaks into it)
          6:15. Mice and gerbils are acting
          rather strangely...

                    FLOATING LIGHT(V.O.)
          They're having sex.

                    KELLY
          Oh God! You're still here?!

                    FLOATING LIGHT
          Of course. We can't leave, remember?

                    KELLY
          But where'd you go before? And where
          are you now?

                    FLOATING LIGHT(reappearing)
          Right here. We didn't leave. We have
          the power of transenmaterial soarcon.

                    KELLY
          What?

                    FLOATING LIGHT
          You call it invisibility.

                    KELLY
               (looking out window)
          Oh, wow! So you're spaceship is still
          there also, only it's invisible.
          This is so cool. And what did you do
          to my animals. I've never seen them
          act this way before.

                    FLOATING LIGHT
          We didn't do anything. They got some
          of Hormonious on them. You invented,
          what we think you call,... the
          ultimate aphrodisiac.

                    KELLY
              (looking back at
               animals)
         No shit?! And they drank some....?

                    KELLY'S SISTER
              (upstairs, o.s.)
         No, we can't. My parents are upstairs.

                    KELLY'S BOYFRIEND(o.s.)
         So, we go downstairs. Come on.

                    KELLY
              (hearing approaching
               footsteps)
         O-oh. Quick, ah. We can't be down
         here.

                    FLOATING LIGHT
         Okay.

In a flash of light, the floating light is gone (invisible)
and so is Kelly! She is still holding the tape recorder which
is now floating in the air in her invisible hand. She sees
the floating tape recorder.

                    KELLY(invisible)
         Holy shit!

She lets go of the tape recorder. It falls to the floor.

                    KELLY (CONT'D)
         Where am I?

                    FLOATING LIGHT(invisible)
         You said we shouldn't be here so we
         made you and us...

                    KELLY
         ...invisible. I get it.
              (basement door starts
               to open)
         Shhh!

CHRISTIE BROWN enters. She is Kelly's 21 year old sister.
Attractive, proper and high class. She looks around the room.
Her 23 year old boyfriend, **JEFF**, enters behind her. Both
have cokes in their hands.

                    CHRISTIE
         Hello? Kelly, are you down here?

                    JEFF
         There's nobody here.

                    CHRISTIE
         I thought I heard voices.

                    JEFF
          Ms. Psychology Major hearing things.
          That's not a good sign. I think you
          need some medical attention.

Jeff moves forward, kisses her and tries to start unbuttoning
her shirt. Christie pushes him away.

                    CHRISTIE(places coke on counter)
          Not now, Jeff. Especially not here.

                    JEFF
          What's wrong with here? I think this
          place is neat.

                    KELLY
              (invisible, softly)
          Thank-you.

                    CHRISTIE
              (barely hearing her)
          What?

                    JEFF
              (not hearing Kelly)
          I said I thought this place is neat.
          Just look at it. Looks like something
          out of a bad B-movie.

                    CHRISTIE
          Yep. My sister. The crazy little mad
          scientist. She's one who needs some
          serious medical attention.

                    KELLY
          Oh yeah?

                    CHRISTIE
          Oh yeah. Down here all the time. No
          friends, no job, no life...

                    JEFF
              (spotting the animals)
          Hey, look at this! Give you any ideas?

He tries to grab her again. She pulls away.

                    CHRISTIE
          Jeff, stop it. I told you I'm not in
          the mood!

P.O.V. of Kelly- she looks at Jeff and Christie and then
switches her view on the still bubbling bowl of Hormonious.
She walks over to the bowl.

                    JEFF(grabs her again)
               But you're never in the mood. Come
               on, let's play mad scientist...

Christie and Jeff have their backs turned to the lab table.
They don't see a lab spoon suddenly rise in the air. The
spoon dips into the bubbling bowl and fills itself with the
formula. The spoon moves over to Christie's coke can and
pours itself. The spoon then gently lays back on the table.

                    CHRISTIE(pulling away)
               I told you I'm not into kinky things.
               Now just quit it.

                    JEFF
               Alright! But, you know, sex is a
               healthy part of a good relationship.

                    CHRISTIE
                 (grabbing coke can)
               We had sex last month. We shouldn't
               over do it.

Christie takes another gulp from the coke can.

                    KELLY(softly)
               Bottoms up.

                    JEFF
               Don't worry about over doing it.
               That's one thing that people won't
               accuse us of. Well, let's go back
               upstairs. You can watch the sun set
               while I take another cold shower.

Christie finishes her drink. Her eyes suddenly go wide. She
looks down at herself and can feel her body throbbing. She
starts to rub her hands up and down herself. Jeff is turned
away and starting to head for the stairs.

                    CHRISTIE
               Jeff.

                    JEFF
                 (turned away)
               What?

                    CHRISTIE
                 (rubbing faster)
               Jeff!

                    JEFF
                 (turning)
               What?!

                    CHRISTIE
               (turned on to say the
                least)
          This is what!

Christie rips her shirt wide open and starts to undo her pants. Jeff is surprised and confused.

                    JEFF
          Christie, what are you doing?

                    CHRISTIE
               (pulling down her
                pants)
          You have to ask?

                    JEFF
               (realizing)
          No, I suppose not.
               (Christie pops her
                bra open revealing
                her attractive figure)
          Oh my! Hey, let's do this slow and
          romantic-like.

                    CHRISTIE
          Fuck that!

Christie leaps forwards and grabs the crotch of his pants. She pulls them off, tackles Jeff to the ground, jumps on top of him and...

                    KELLY
          Go to it, sis!

                    JEFF
          What? You hear something?

                    CHRISTIE
          Just shut up!

She plants a big kiss on his lips and rips the rest of his clothes off. They start having mad, passionate, lustful sex.

The coke can then quietly lifts off the table and tilts a little.

                    KELLY(invisible, looking in can)
          Strong stuff.

                                                  CUT TO:

INT. KEN'S HOUSE - BEDROOM - DUSK.

Ken comes out of the closet in his pajamas.

MARTIN
What's this?

KEN
I think its a bad idea to go out when one is hallucinating. I'm just going to spend a quiet night here.

MARTIN
But it's only six.

KEN
(climbing into bed)
I know. Rest. I need a lot of rest.

DOORBELL RINGS. Martin and Ken turn towards the sound.

MARTIN
Rest, huh?

KEN
(climbing out of bed)
Who could that be?

CUT TO:

EXT. KEN'S HOUSE - DUSK.

Jenny is standing by the front door. She is not happy. Ken and Martin walk towards it. They see her.

MARTIN
Dan's girlfriend. Are you crazy? You stud.

KEN
(behind glass door)
Hi, Jenny.

JENNY
I have a message from Dan.

KEN
I know. I'm dead.

JENNY
He says you're dead.

KEN
The surprises don't stop.

MARTIN
What does he say about me?

                    JENNY
                (confused)
            Ah, I don't know. I don't remember
            him saying anything about you.

                    MARTIN
                (opening front door
                 to leave)
            That's all I wanted to hear. Gotta
            go, pal. Write down the grave. I'll
            send flowers.

                    KEN
            Thanks.

As the door opens wide, Jenny smells something in the air.
She sniffs it deeply and takes another look at Ken.

                    MARTIN(to Jenny)
            Can I walk you back to your car?

                    JENNY
                (smelling air)
            No, I want...
                (moves towards Ken)
            I want to...can I use your bathroom?

                    KEN
            Death threats and bathroom favors.
            Sure. Why not?

Jenny walks inside the house and past Ken. Ken waves good-
bye to Martin.

                    MARTIN(smiling)
            Well, if you're gonna die, might as
            well go out with a bang.

                    KEN
            See you tomorrow.

Ken closes the door as Martin walks away.

                                                    CUT TO:

INT. KEN'S HOUSE - DOWNSTAIRS - DUSK.

Ken turns to Jenny.

                    KEN (CONT'D)
            The bathroom's right down the hall...

Jenny has other things on her mind.

                    JENNY
            I like those pajamas you're wearing.

                    KEN
               (cautious)
          Yeah? Thanks.

                    JENNY
               (rubbing up against
                him)
          You know, I always liked you, Kenny?

                    KEN
          No, you didn't. In ninth grade, you
          threw a rock at me. In tenth grade,
          you laughed when Dan pushed me down
          the stairs...

                    JENNY
          Well, I want to make-up.

Jenny plants a big kiss on Ken's lips. He jumps back.

                    KEN
          What are you trying to pull here?

                    JENNY
               (advancing)
          I just want to pull you...closer.

Jenny reaches out for Ken. Ken jumps back. Jenny begins to undress.

                    KEN
          Oh no. I'm not falling for this.
          You're just trying to get me to make
          a fool out of myself. Seduce me into
          getting dressed up in a pink tu-tu
          or something like that so everyone
          can have a big laugh.

Jenny steps out of her jeans. She is wearing very-revealing panties.

                    JENNY
          I just want you to take your clothes
          off.

                    KEN
          A-ha! I knew it. Then you pull out
          a camera and next thing I know, my
          naked picture is plastered all over
          the school.

                    JENNY
               (pulling off her top)
          I don't want a picture of you. I
          want <u>you</u>!

                        KEN
                    (jumping away)
                Until Dan suddenly bursts in and
                beats my face in. No, it's not going
                to work! I'm not an idiot.

                        VOICE(in corner)
                Yes, you are.

                        KEN
                Who said that?

Ken turns and sees the cat sitting on a chair. Jenny pushes
Ken on to a sofa and climb on top of him. She rips open Ken's
pajama top and starts kissing Ken' chest.

                        KEN (CONT'D)
                Oh. Don't...Ah...okay. I give up.
                Take me.

Jenny looks up at him and smiles. She sees the cat and
sneezes.

                        JENNY
                A cat. I'm allergic to cats. I get
                all...stuffed...

Jenny sneezes again. Her nose gets stuffed and can no longer
smell Ken's scent. She sits up and shakes her head. She looks
down at Ken and screams at the sight of herself naked on top
of Ken.

                        JENNY(jumping off) (CONT'D)
                AHHH! YOU...YOU...!!
                    (grabs her clothes)
                You're really dead now!

Jenny quickly gets dressed and runs out of the house. Ken
flops back on the sofa.

                        KEN
                I'll never understand women.

                                                CUT TO:

INT. KELLY'S HOUSE - LIVING ROOM - EARLY EVENING.

The front door opens and Christie's two very attractive female
European pen pals enter. They have some shopping bags. They
are talking with themselves when they hear.

                        JEF(o.s.)
                No more. Enough! Later. We'll do it
                again later.

                        CHRISTIE(o.s.)
                Couldn't you make it sooner?

The basement door open and Jeff and Christie come out. Jeff is trying to zip up his pants. Christie can't take her hands off him.

                    CHRISTIE(still grabbing Jeff) (CONT'D)
    Hi, Monique. Shawnee. Have a fun day
    exploring the city?

                    MONIQUE(with accent)
    Yes.

Christie pushes Jeff upstairs to her bedroom, grabbing him all over.

                    CHRISTIE
    That's nice. Good-night.

                    JEFF
    Couldn't we have some dinner, first?

                    CHRISTIE
    No!

Jeff and Christie disappear upstairs. **Monique** and **Shawnee** turn to each other.

                    MONIQUE
    And they always say we French girls
    are so sex-crazed.

                                            CUT TO:

INT. BASEMENT LAB - EVENING.

The basement door closes by itself. There is suddenly a burst of light and the floating light and Kelly reappear. Kelly is jumping up and down.

                    KELLY
    This is great! Boy, is she going to
    feel guilty in the morning. I love
    it. She hates sex.

                    FLOATING LIGHT
    Not anymore. And your friend, Ken is
    going to be in for a big surprise
    tomorrow.

                    KELLY
    What do you mean?

                    FLOATING LIGHT
    Hormonious is permanent.

                                              CUT TO:

INT. KEN'S HOUSE - NEXT DAY.

ROCK MUSIC comes up from the radio. Ken is in bed sleeping for a second. The music wakes him up. He sits up and looks around. Everything seems normal. He smiles and gets out of bed.

MUSIC continues to play over a quick MONTAGE of Ken getting dressed and ready for school. He goes to the kitchen and looks at his list of things to do.

C.U. of list- which reads "1) Do laundry." This is followed by quick shot of laundry being throw into washing machine.

C.U. of item one being checked off and pan down to "2) Do dishes." This is followed by a full dishwasher being closed and turned on.

C.U. of item two checked off and pan down to "3) Feed Hemburn's dogs."

Ken drops his head, not pleased about this final task.

                                        CUT TO:

EXT. KEN'S HOUSE - MORNING.

Ken walks outside with his school books. It is a beautiful sunny day outside. Ken takes a deep breath and then realizes something.

            KEN(in driveway, to himself)
        No car. Wonderful.

He walks over to the neighbors house next door.

                                        CUT TO:

EXT. HEMBURN'S HOUSE - MORNING.

Ken unlocks and slowly opens the front door. Ken peeks his head inside.

            KEN(announcing) (CONT'D)
        It's just me. The next door neighbor
        who's supposed to keep you gals alive
        while your owners and my parents
        have a good time in Florida. Remember
        me? I'm coming in to feed you so
        don't attack!

Ken walks into the house and closes the door behind him.

WE HEAR two Doberman Pinchers run growling towards Ken.

            KEN(from inside) (CONT'D)
        Oh no. Not again.

SOUNDS OF SLURPING AND PANTING IS HEARD INSIDE.

Ken bursts out the front door and slams it behind him. His hair is all messed up, his clothes are in disarray and he's covered with dog hair. His face is covered with dog saliva. He catches his breath and hears the dogs scratching on the other side of the door.

                    KEN (CONT'D)
They were friendly this morning.

Ken looks up to see his car waiting in front of his house. It is running. His car horn suddenly honks. Ken runs over to the car to find Hormonious, in perfect woman form, behind the wheel.

                    HORMONIOUS(happily)
'Morning. Hop in.

                    KEN(upset)
Oh no. No, no, no, no, no, no, no, no,.... No.

                    HORMONIOUS
So you're saying you don't want to hop in?

                    KEN
No! Get out. Out of my car. Now.

She does and Ken starts to get in his car.

                    HORMONIOUS
That's not very nice. Especially since I helped you with that girl last night.

                    KEN
Helped?

                    HORMONIOUS
The cat. Stuffed nose. You didn't want her. I helped. Personally, I thought she was attractive but different tastes.

                    KEN
      (getting control)
I am not listening to this. I don't listen to people who don't exist.

                    HORMONIOUS
Sure I exist. You existed me!

                              KEN
                 I did not exist...I did not invent
                 you. I invented a puddle of goop.
                 And since you're not a puddle of
                 goop, you're not real. So anything
                 you say or tell me is not real. Now,
                 excuse me, you unreal fantasy. I'm
                 going to school to get beat up and
                 hopefully get some sense kicked into
                 me.

                              HORMONIOUS
                 What about the way the dogs acted?

                              KEN
                 Dogs and women are two very different
                 beings even though the expression
                 sometimes overlaps. Good-bye.

He drives off.

                              HORMONIOUS(calling after him)
                 But they're all going to act the
                 same way!

Ken's car drives down the road. Hormonious, as the woman, stands there and watches him go.

                                                  CUT TO:

INT. MS. PUDDLE'S CLASSROOM - DAY.

All the students are talking and making their way to their seats. Ms. Puddle is writing some notes on the blackboard.

Dan notices Ken's empty seat and walks over to Jenny.

                              DAN
                 So, the little coward decided not to
                 show up today. I guess you gave him
                 my message.

                              JENNY
                     (mumbling)
                 I gave him more than that.

                              DAN
                 What do you mean?

                              JENNY
                 I don't want to talk about it.
                 Just get him good if he shows up.

The final bell RINGS. Everyone takes their seats. Ms. Puddle goes to close the door when Ken bursts in, breathing hard. Ms. Puddle looks a bit annoyed until she gets a whiff of his odor.

                    KEN
          Sorry. I was unavoidably detained.

                    MS PUDDLE
                (smiling)
          That's okay. Take your seat.

Ken moves to his seat that is smack in the middle of the
classroom. He glances over at Dan, Brad, Bart, Biff and Gino.
They watch Ken sit down with "kill-you" faces. Dan quietly
mouths, "You're dead".

Ms. Puddle starts to teach. Ken looks over to the other side
of him to see Jenny and her gang of girls. They are not mad
anymore but licking their lips. Ken realizes he is in a bad
position. The girls are slowly inching their chairs closer
to Ken.

Ms. Puddle is also staring at Ken as she continues trying to
teach but is having a hard time. She rubs the pointing stick
against her body. She teaches directly to Ken as she slides
her skirt up a bit and unbuttons her blouse during the course
of the lesson.

One girl slides over to Ken in her chair. She reaches out
and squeezes his thigh.

Ken jumps and slides his desk/chair away from her. More girls
smell his scent and start sliding up to him. Ken slides away
and notices he's heading towards Dan and his gang.

Ken slides his desk forwards. Dan and his gang slide their
desk/chairs after him.

Pretty soon, everybody in the class is moving their chairs
towards Ken. The girls want to seduce him and the guys want
to bash his brains in.

Ken is forced to slide closer and closer to Ms Puddle and
the blackboard. The closer Ken gets, the stronger his odor
becomes. Ms. Puddle rubs her hands up and down the pointing
stick faster and faster. She finally drops her stick right
by Ken's feet.

Ms. Puddle smiles at him and bends down to pick it up. Her
head disappears under Ken's desk.

Everybody is closing in from every direction. Ken then hears
his pants UNZIP! He looks down and see Ms. Puddle's hands
are where they shouldn't be.

Ken bursts up out of his seat as many hands reach out.

                    KEN
          I have to go to the bathroom!!

                                                  CUT TO:

INT. BATHROOM - DAY.

Ken enters and takes a breath. He walks over to one of the sinks, turns on the faucet and splashes water on his face. He feels a little better and looks over at the sink next to him.

A big wide **SNAKE** is in the sink looking at him! The snake flicks its tongue out. Ken screams and jumps back.

In a second, the snake turns into the perfect woman form. Hormonious jumps out of the sink.

                    HORMONIOUS
          Relax. Don't like snakes, huh?

                    KEN
          You again?! What the hell is happening
          around here? Those girls.
          They...they...

                    HORMONIOUS
          ...They smell me on you. I've been
          trying to explain it to you.
          Externally, I turn-on others.
          Internally, I turn-on you....To put
          it simply, you've created the most
          powerful aphrodisiac ever.

                    KEN
          But...But I don't even like sex.

                    HORMONIOUS
             (short pause)
          Learn.

                    KEN
          Oh, you're a big help. Just turn
          back into a snake and slither away.
          I have to figure out what to do.

                    HORMONIOUS
          But I prefer this form. Long shapely
          legs, nice ass....
             (she rubs her hands
              over herself as she
              talks)
          ....smooth stomach, great chest...
             (pulls off her bikini
              top and rubs them)
          ...luscious lips...
             (licks her lips and
              sniffs the air)
          God, I even turn myself on....How
          about you, Kenny?
                    (MORE)

                    HORMONIOUS (CONT'D)
                (moving towards him)
            After all, I am your dream girl.
            Haven't you always wanted to make it
            with your dream girl?

She backs Ken into a corner. She reaches out and gently grabs Ken's hands.

                    HORMONIOUS:
            Let me guide you.

Hormonious moves Ken's hands on to her body. She slowly moves them over her entire figure. Ken is too in shock to stop her.

Hormonious moves one of his hands around to her ass and moves his other hand up to her mouth. She seductively starts sucking on his fingers.

                    HORMONIOUS (pulling away for a second)
            Well?

                    KEN
            Very...educational.

                    HORMONIOUS
            Want to learn more?

Ken can't respond.

                    HORMONIOUS (CONT'D)
            I just have to go to the bathroom
            first.

                    KEN
            We're in the bathroom.

Hormonious moves towards an open stall.

                    HORMONIOUS
            Good. Then it shouldn't take long.

                    KEN
            But this is the boys bathroom!

                    HORMONIOUS
            Okay. That's simple enough.

In a flash, Hormonious turns back into the male body builder in the skimpy bathing suit and enters the stall. He closes the door behind him. Ken slowly lets his head drop against the wall.

                    KEN
            What am I doing?
                    (MORE)

                    KEN (CONT'D)
          I'm letting my creation get the best
          of me. How could it get any worse?

Suddenly the bathroom door bursts open and Dan enters. Ken jumps.

                    DAN
          Well, well. I've been waiting for
          this moment for quite some time now.

                    KEN
          Dan. What a pleasant surprise!
          There's nothing I can do to avoid
          this beating, is there?

Dan, moving forwards, shakes his head.

                    KEN (CONT'D)
          Okay. Just try to keep the hits in
          the body area, please.

Ken closes his eyes and waits for impact. Dan swings his fist back. The toilet then flushes. Dan turns to the stall. Ken opens his eyes.

Hormonious, the body builder, walks out. He looks at Ken and Dan.

                    HORMONIOUS
          Oh, am I interrupting anything?

                    DAN
              (lowering fist)
          Who...who is this?!

                    KEN
              (relaxing and smiling)
          Oh, Dan. I'm sorry. Forget to
          introduce you. Dan, this is my good
          friend, Hormonious.

                    DAN:
              (backing up to door)
          Pleased to meet you. I'll be back,
          Ken. I'll be back.

Dan runs out the bathroom door. Ken smiles as he watches him run.

Ken looks back to Hormonious.

                    KEN
          Thanks.

                    HORMONIOUS
          No problem. Want me to escort you
          back to class?

                    KEN
               (smiling)
          I don't think that would be such a
          great idea. Something you can do
          though. Get this scent off me?

                    HORMONIOUS
          Sorry. No can do.

                    KEN
          Why not?

                    HORMONIOUS
          I'm permanent.

                    KEN
               (losing smile)
          Permanent permanent? Never come off?

                    HORMONIOUS
          That's right.

                    KEN
               (smiling again)
          Could you turn back into that cat
          again? Please.

                    HORMONIOUS
               (confused)
          Okay.

In a flash, Hormonious is a cat. Ken's smile then disappears.

Ken charges at the cat.

                    KEN
          Permanent, huh?! I'm going to kill
          you!!

The cat run around room. Ken chases after it. The cat meows
as it races across the tile floor.

                    KEN (CONT'D)
          Come back here!! Come on. Let me
          show you something permanent!!!

Ken continues to chase the cat around the bathroom. The cat
runs under one of the sinks. Ken runs after it and smashes
his head against the sink!

BLACKNESS.

                                                  CUT TO:

INT. BEDROOM - DAY - DREAM.

C.U. of Ken's face. He smiles. CAMERA slowly pulls back to reveal that he is laying on a huge king-size bed. An **ATTRACTIVE WOMAN** is laying next to him on the right, dressed in seductive lingerie.

                    ATTRACTIVE WOMAN 1
        That was great.

She kisses him. CAMERA continues to pull back to reveal **another ATTRACTIVE WOMAN** on the other side of him. She strokes his cheek.

                    ATTRACTIVE WOMAN 2
        You were so good.

CAMERA continues to pull back to reveal the entire bed is filled with beautiful women in lingerie. All compliment Ken on his lovemaking skills.

CAMERA continues to pull back as suddenly all the **BOYFRIENDS** and **HUSBANDS** of the women surround the bed. They don't look very happy.

                    HUSBAND 1
        That's my wife you just slept with!

                    BOYFRIEND 1
        And that's _my_ girlfriend!

The rest chime in on the fact. They raise their fists as they approach Ken.

Ken screams as CAMERA quickly zooms back towards Ken and ends at a E.C.U. of Ken's screaming mouth.

                                        CUT TO:

INT. NURSE'S OFFICE- DAY.

Ken wakes up and sits up. He is laying on a cot. Ms. Puddle is looking over him as is a big-busted **NURSE** in a nurse uniform.

                    KEN
        What is it? Where am I? What
        happened?!

                    MS. PUDDLE
        Relax. Everything is fine. You had
        an accident and smashed your head.
        I brought you to the nurse.

                    KEN
        I hit my head? I knew it!! It was a
        dream. It was all just a dream!

                    MS PUDDLE
                (standing up)
            Yes. It was just a dream.

Ken takes a sigh of relief and looks down at himself to
discover that he is completely naked except for his underwear.
                    KEN(shocked, looks up at nurse)
            What happened to my clothes?

                    MS. PUDDLE
            Don't worry. You won't be needing
            them.

                    NURSE
            You are suffering from a severe case
            of stress and tension. You must be
            relieved of this state. There is
            only one cure.

The **NURSE** strips off her uniform to reveal a S&M RUBBER outfit
underneath complete with whips and chains.

Ms. Puddle strips of her dress as well to reveal black leather
outfit and silk stockings underneath.

                    KEN
            Oh God! It wasn't a dream.

Ms. Puddle and the nurse leap at Ken, who throws himself off
the cot, just dodges them.

(ROCK MUSIC plays throughout the following SEQUENCE.)

Ms. Puddle lands on the cot and starts to move off towards
Ken.

Ken quickly rolls under the cot and gets up on the other
side as Ms. Puddle hits the floor. The nurse advances. Ken
jumps under her legs as she grabs for him. The nurse misses
and tumbles forwards into Ms. Puddle.

Ken sees his clothes laying in a bundle on a table. He grabs
them and flies out the door as the nurse and Ms. Puddle get
up.

                    MS. PUDDLE
            Come back! I want you!!!

                    NURSE
            You must learn discipline!

                                                    CUT TO:

INT.   HALLWAYS - DAY.

Class is still in session so the hallways are empty. Ken creeps down the hall in his underwear. He reaches a corner and peeks around it. The coast is clear.

Ken starts to put his pants on when the bell rings. Ken falls to the floor, trying to put one leg in. Ken jumps up and looks for a place to hide.

He is standing in the center of the hall, with no place to go as all the students pile out of their summer school classes.

All the students stop and look at Ken. Ken notices a familiar look starting to stir in the girls. There is a moment of silence.

>   KEN:(smiling for a second)
> And for my next trick....AHHHHH!!!!

Ken pulls his pants up and bursts into a run down the hall. The girls are right behind him!

A couple of girls try to cut him off but with some incredibly slick dodges, slides, and flips, he gets past all of them.

Ken and the mob run past Martin who jumps to the side and watches them pass.

>   MARTIN(to himself)
> The cat was right.

>   KEN
> HORMONIOUS!!!!

Ken screams as he runs down the hall pursued by an army of high school girls, some of which are ripping their clothes off as they chase.

Ken reaches the end of one hall that has a sign that says, "Careful. Wet floor".

Ken doesn't stop and slides for about fifty feet across the floor and smashes through the big swinging doors at the end.

>   CUT TO:

INT. GYM - DAY.

Ken slides straight through the doors across the floor and into a corner.

The girls burst into the gym. They approach. Ken is trapped.

>   KEN:(looking at the oncoming army)
> This could get ugly.

Suddenly Dan pushes his way past everyone else. He makes a fist and looks at Ken.

                    DAN
     He's mine.

Dan is then grabbed by about twenty girls, picked up, and thrown backwards across the room.

                    KEN
     Thanks, girls.

They turn back to Ken and continue to approach. Ken is against a wall.

                SQUEAKY VOICE(low)
     Need any help?

Ken looks down and sees Hormonious in the shape of a little mouse next to him. The mouse looks up at him.

                    KEN
     Hormonious?

                HORMONIOUS
     You betcha. How can I help?

                    KEN
     I don't know. How can you help?

                HORMONIOUS
     Um, give me a second.

In a flash the mouse turns into a huge **OCTOPUS**! The octopus swings its tentacles at the crowd of girls. The girls take a step back but are still determined.

                KEN(to Hormonious)
     Better but I don't think that's going
     to stop them.

                HORMONIOUS
     Only one thing to do then.

The girls start to move closer. The octopus raises its tentacles and squirts gallons of "colored water" from it's spores!

The girls are sent flying backwards like being hit with a fire hose. Ken watches as girls, girls and more girls fall over each other, get up, and tumble back again. There are more wet T-shirts that one can imagine.

                KEN(yelling to Hormonious)
     Great! That water should cool them
     down for a while.

                    HORMONIOUS
               (still firing)
          I'm not made up of water! You should
          know that by now!

                    KEN
               (realizing)
          Oh, you didn't?!!

                    HORMONIOUS
          They didn't come up with the
          expression "Raging Hormones" from
          nowhere!!!

Ken watches as girls and guys covered with the jello-like
slime get up and fall down again.

                    KEN(shocked)
          Oh my God! This is going to turn
          into...

                    HORMONIOUS
          ...The biggest orgy you've ever seen!
          And it's never going to end!!

Ken watches in horror as the formula starts to take affect.
The girls start ripping off the guys clothes. The guys start
ripping off the girl's clothes. Teachers are involved too.

CAMERA zooms into a tight shot of Ken's face. A look of horror
overtakes his face.

                    KEN
          What did I do? What did I create? I
          was trying to control hormones and
          I've created a sexual apocalypse!
          This could destroy the world!

                    HORMONIOUS
          Yeah, but everyone will have a lot
          of fun in the process. Just goes to
          show you. Never fool with Mother
          Nature.

                    KEN
          I got to stop it. There's got to be
          some way to stop it!

Ken runs out of the gym by the first door he sees as the
orgy gets into full swing with the octopus helping some of
the students off with their clothes.

                                             CUT TO:

INT. GIRL'S SHOWER ROOM - DAY.

Ken runs through to the exit. He realizes where he is and stops short. Around 10 naked or almost naked girls freeze and look at him. They are upset until they smell him. They smile.

                  KEN(smiles back)
Ah, more naked girls. How you doing? Don't mind me. I'm just passing through.
    (he turns to the CAMERA)
And I bet you thought we had forgotten the obligatory girls locker room scene.

Ken turns away and runs out of the shower as the naked girls approach.

                              CUT TO:

EXT. KELLY'S HOUSE - DAY - LATER.

Ken runs over to the front door and begins to knock and yell.

                  KEN (CONT'D)
Kelly!!...Kelly, It's Ken.!!! Kelly! ...Kelly!!

No answer. Ken runs around to the back of the house.

                              CUT TO:

EXT. KELLY'S BACKYARD - DAY.

                  KEN (CONT'D)
KELLY!!...KELLY!!!....KEL....

Ken comes running around the back of the house when he suddenly hits something, although nothing can be seen. A loud CLANG rings out as Ken falls to the grass.

Ken is dazed. He shakes his head, trying to come to. He then hears a yell upstairs. One of the upstairs windows open and Jeff sticks his head out.

                  JEFF(begging)
Help me!! Please, God. Help me!! She's locked me up here!! She won't stop!... She won't...

Suddenly Jeff is pulled away from the window. Ken starts to get up.

                  CHRISTIE
Come back here. You want kinky?!
    (MORE)

CHRISTIE (CONT'D)
Bark like a dog for me while I ride you.

She reaches over to close the window. Ken sees her.

KEN
Christine! Hey, Hi. Is Kelly home?!

CHRISTIE
(seeing him)
No. I think she went to your house. Hey, want to come up here and join us?

KEN
What are you doing?

CHRISTIE
Oh. just some...anatomical research.

JEFF
NOOO!! SAVE YOURSELF!!!

CHRISTIE
Shut up, slave!

KEN
Ah, no thanks. Maybe later.

CHRISTIE
No? Then leave us alone!

JEFF
No, no! PLEASSSSEEE....

The window is slammed shut and the voices get muffled inside. Ken quickly runs off to his house.

CUT TO:

INT. KEN'S HOUSE - KEN'S BEDROOM - MINUTES LATER

P.O.V. of someone entering room and looking around. Nobody's there.

KELLY
Visibility, please.

There is a quick flash and suddenly Kelly and the floating light appear. She turns and looks up at the light.

KELLY (CONT'D)
Where'd he go?

FLOATING LIGHT
Don't know.

                    KELLY
          He wouldn't be stupid enough to try
          to go to school today? Or would he?

The sound of the downstairs door slamming open is heard!

                    KEN(O.S.)
          Kelly?!

                    KELLY
               (calling down)
          I'm upstairs!

Ken bursts into his room. The floating light is in the corner of the room. Ken doesn't even see it when he comes in.

                    KEN(starting to babble)
          Kelly, I can't believe what we've
          done. Everything's out of control. I
          mean, just yesterday everything was
          peaceful and calm. I'd go to school,
          come home, do my homework, go to
          bed. It was dull but it was okay.
          But now...now I take a shower with
          naked ladies, yell at and try to
          kill cats, escape via talking horse
          from sex-crazed restaurant workers.
          This is not my idea of a good time!...

Kelly is trying to concentrate on what Ken is saying but his scent is really starting to get to her.

                    KEN(pacing) (CONT'D)
          ...And now I've just started a world-
          wide sex craze that can't be stopped.
          At least, occurring to Hormonious.

                    FLOATING LIGHT
          That's true. Once the chemical
          combines with the body sweat, there
          is no reversing the effect.

                    KEN
               (glancing at the light
                while he passes)
          Great. Thanks a lot. So now Kelly,
          the...
               (looks back at light)
          You're still here? Oh, yeah. You
          can't take off. Is your ship invisible
          in Kelly's backyard?

                    FLOATING LIGHT
          Yes.

                    KEN
          Well, I think I dented it with my
          head. Anyway, Kelly. What are we
          going to do?!

                    KELLY
               (moving towards him)
          You know what I think we should do?

                    KEN
          What

                    KELLY
               (very hot)
          Fuck!!

She grabs Ken. He pushes her away. She starts unbuttoning
her shirt.

                    KEN
          Oh no. Not you too?!

                    KELLY
               (undressing)
          Come on, Ken. Let's have a little
          fun.

                    KEN
               (grabbing baseball
                bat)
          Kelly, I'm warning you. I know how
          to use this.

                    KELLY:
               (dropping shirt and
                working on bra)
          You want to play? Okay.
               (to floating light)
          Transenmaterial soarcon, please.

                    FLOATING LIGHT
          You've got it.

Kelly pops open her bra and in a flash, Kelly and the floating
light disappears! The bra falls to the floor. Ken looks around
the room, confused.

                    KEN
          What the....Where'd you go?

He hears giggling and then suddenly the zipper on his pants
unzip as the button pops open.

                    KEN(dropping bat) (CONT'D)
          Holy shit!

Ken's pants start to slide down. He tries to pull them back up.

                    KEN (CONT'D)
          Kelly. Stop it!! Kelly...Kelly!!

Ken tries to run but she has him by the back of the pants.

He pulls hard and falls flat down on his face. He then hears another unzipping sound and more laughter.

He watches as his legs are raised and pants slid off.

Ken tries to crawl away when invisible Kelly grabs him and throws him on top of the bed. He then feels her jump on top of him. He fights to keep his shirt on.

                    KEN (CONT'D)
          No. Kelly, no. I'm...
          not...going...to...

She throws his head back on the pillow. RIP!! Ken watches his underwear fly across the room. Ken tries to push Kelly away.

His hands press against her invisible body. One hand squeezes something.

                    KEN(feeling it in his hand) (CONT'D)
          What's this?

                    KELLY
              (invisible, teasing)
          What do you think?!

Ken quickly retracts his hand. He and the bed are starting to shake and bounce up and down. He can hear Kelly starting to moan.

                    KELLY (CONT'D)
          Oh yes...yes..uh-huh, that's
          It....oooohhhh...ahhhhh....

                    KEN
              (bouncing on his back)
          I was wrong. Invisible sex crazed
          women. It has gotten worse....well,
          this is certainly different.

Ken and the bed start bouncing higher and faster. Kelly moans louder. Suddenly, Ken hears footsteps.

                    MARTIN(o.s.)
          Ken! You here? You won't believe
          what's going on....

                    KEN(softly)
          Stop. Stop...Kelly, ahh....

Kelly is too much into it. Ken quickly grabs one of the
pillows and holds it in front of his and Kelly's invisible
private area.

Martin bursts into the room.

                    MARTIN
          Ken, what I've seen going on at....
              (sees Ken laying on
               his back and bouncing
               up and down on bed)
          What are you doing?

                    KEN
              (looking up at him
               and breathing heavy)
          Doing?....Ah, I...I'm...

                    MARTIN
          What is this? Some kind of new type
          of exercise?

                    KEN
              (still bouncing)
          Exercise?...Yeah, In a way...sort
          of....

                    MARTIN
          Well, can you stop that? I want to
          tell you what's happening at
          school...Are you completely naked?

                    KEN
          Yeah. It's important in the exercise.
          Ken...Ahh, yes, uh-huh...I'm finishing
          up now....

                    KELLY
          Yes, now!

                    KEN:
              (jumping in with her)
          YES. Now!...Now, I'm going to finish.
          Could you...ohhh...could you wait
          outside for a minute?

                    MARTIN
              (very confused)
          Sure. I'll be right out there.

                    KEN
               (bouncing faster and
                faster)
          Actually, could...co...cou...could
          you get me a glass of water from
          downstairs? .....I....I....I could
          really use it.

                    MARTIN
          Okay. Yeah. You do look a little red
          in the face.

                    KEN
               (sweating)
          Really?!

Martin walks out of the room as Ken squeezes the pillow
tightly. Moaning gets louder and more intense.

                                        CUT TO:

INT. HALL - OUTSIDE KEN'S BEDROOM DOOR - DAY.

Martin pauses for a second to listen at the increasing moans
and screams. Martin cocks his head and then heads downstairs.

                                        CUT TO:

INT. KEN'S BEDROOM - DAY.

Ken is trying to catch his breath. He and the bed stop
bouncing for a second.

                    KELLY
          That was great. Let's do it again!

Suddenly Ken and the bed start to move again.

                    KEN
          Oh no. No. Kelly. He's...Martin's
          ....Hey, space light!

                    FLOATING LIGHT
          Yes?

                    KEN
          Could you do something about her for
          a little while.

                    FLOATING LIGHT
          We can't reverse the affect.

                    KEN
          Just put her out!

Suddenly a red beam of light shoot out of the air and hits
Kelly!

A naked outline of her body can be seen for a second until the light disappears. Ken feels her collapse on top of him. The bed stops moving.

                    KEN(trying to push her off him) (CONT'D)
          Ohhh. What did you do?

                    FLOATING LIGHT
          Nothing. She's just going to take a
          little nap.

He manages to pry himself out from underneath her. Her invisible body flops to the side and lays still on the bed.

Ken throws a blanket around himself as he gets up.

                    KEN(looking at empty bed)
          Jeez, Kelly. You could lose a little
          weight, you know.

Martin comes back in with the glass of water. He gives Ken the water.

                    KEN (CONT'D)
          Thanks.

                    MARTIN
              (moving to sit on bed)
          That's an interesting exercise you've
          got there.

                    KEN
          NO!! DON'T SIT THERE!!!

                    MARTIN
              (jumping up)
          Okay. I'm sorry. I'll just stand up
          right here then, okay?

                    KEN
          Okay, good. So, what's up?

                    MARTIN
          What's up? What's up!?...What isn't
          up?! I want to know what you started
          at the school. It's a madhouse down
          there! First you're being chased by
          every female in the area. Then an
          octopus appears...an OCTOPUS in the
          middle of the gym blowing snot out
          of its tentacles! And the next thing
          I know all the students and teachers
          are ripping their clothes off and
          screwing anything that moves.

MARTIN (CONT'D)
When I left, there was a porno company setting up down there to shoot an epic. Now, I don't know about you but it sure doesn't seem like a typical summer school Wednesday to me!!

With that Martin plops down on the bed and Kelly!

Martin feels her under him and leaps up, surprised!

MARTIN (CONT'D)
Yeow! What the hell is that?

KEN
(giving up)
That's Kelly.

MARTIN
What's Kelly?

KEN
What you felt on the bed. It's her. Sleeping and invisible.

MARTIN
(moving his hand over her form)
And naked?

KEN
Yep.

MARTIN
(pulling hand away)
Ah, Ken. Out of all those girls at school you pick Kelly? Does she have a good body?

KEN
I don't know! She's invisible.

MARTIN
Well, lets make her visible and see.

KEN
I don't believe you. I just tell you that invisibility is a reality and all you care about is seeing her naked! You don't even care how or who or...

MARTIN
Oh, you mean I walked in while you two were...oh, shit. I'm sorry about that. But how was I to know?

KEN
Martin...

MARTIN
...You mean you had sex with her and don't even know what she looks like?....

KEN
Martin!...

MARTIN
Well, I can see how that could be a plus...

KEN
(fed-up)
MARTIN! Listen, we've got a serious problem here!...

MARTIN
(still with other
 subject)
Sex with an invisible girl. I'm proud of you, Ken. I've never tried that before.

KEN
Okay, look. I've got to figure this out. Help me bring Kelly back to her house. I've got to find a cure.
(looks up at ceiling)
You guys coming, right?

FLOATING LIGHT
We will follow you.

KEN
(grabbing Kelly
 invisible legs)
Good.

MARTIN
Who's that?

KEN
Aliens from an alternate universe.

MARTIN
And they're invisible too?

                        KEN
          Right.

                        MARTIN
                  (grabbing Kelly's
                   invisible arms)
          Hey, I'm starting to get the hang of
          this.

                                                  CUT TO:

INT. KELLY'S HOUSE - EARLY EVENING.

Ken and Martin come in through front door. Both are hunched
over and moving slowly while they carry invisible Kelly. She
moans a few times, starting to come to.

                        KELLY
          Wha... Where am I?

                        KEN
          We brought you home.

                        KELLY
          Oh,...I feel cold.

                        KEN
          Well, you're still naked.

                        KELLY
          Why didn't you get my clothes?

                        KEN
                  (short pause)
          We couldn't find them.

Kelly starts to giggle.

                        KEN (CONT'D)
          Funny, funny, huh?

Ken lets go of her. A loud THUD is heard as she hits the
floor.

                        KEN(heading to basement) (CONT'D)
          Get dressed. I'll meet you downstairs.
          Come on, Martin.

                                                  CUT TO:

INT. BASEMENT LAB- EARLY EVENING.

Martin is watching the news. Ken is pacing back and forth.
The floating light is floating in the corner of the room.

                    NEWS (on television)
　　...As most people know, sex is on
　　the minds of most teen-agers and
　　young adults in America but at Jackson
　　High School, it's more than just on
　　the mind, it's happening and nobody
　　seems to be able to stop it....

There are quick clips of some of the action in the gym. It
blurs to avoid the nudity and sex.

                    NEWS (CONT'D)
　　...At 11:30 this afternoon all the
　　students and faculty seemed to lose
　　all of their inhibitions and clothes
　　in what some have deemed the absolute
　　worst outcome of the causal sex
　　decade. Nobody seems to be able to
　　stop it. Everyone who has entered
　　has just joined in....

                    MARTIN
　　Hey, there's Mindy...Not the back.
　　Show her front!!...Yeah, that's it.
　　Turn around. A little more, little
　　more. NO! Don't cut away!!..Go back!
　　Go back!!....

                    KEN
　　It's the end of the world. We
　　discovered what is probably the
　　biggest scientific finds in history;
　　an alternate universe, real aliens,
　　the power of invisibility; and we
　　have completely perverted it in every
　　possible way.

                    MARTIN
　　Hey, this is America.

                    KEN
　　I lost my virginity to an invisible,
　　aphrodisiac-influenced assistant of
　　mine.

                    MARTIN
　　Well, it's definitely a first....Oh,
　　look! Laura Montandale. She has got
　　the best set of...Oh, and there's
　　Ms. Puddle... Now I know why they
　　chose her to teach biology...

                    KEN
                (to floating light)
　　There's no cure?! Positively no
　　antidote?!

FLOATING LIGHT
Nothing we can come up with and we
are thousands of years more advanced
then your society.

KEN
Then what good are you?! Why are you
even in this picture?!

FLOATING LIGHT
To give Hormonious life.

KEN
Oh, right. Plot points. Plot points.

Suddenly a little spider crawls into the basement through a
small crack between the window and the wall. In a second, it
changes into the perfect woman shape.

HORMONIOUS
Boy! Was that fun! You people talking
about me?

Martin is too busy watching the news report to even notice
her.

KEN
Talking about you?...Why actually we
were. We were talking about how
you....
        (grabs her by the
         throat)
...have just ended hundreds of years
of civilization just for the sake of
having a good time. I invented you.
How could you do this?!....

HORMONIOUS
  (being strangled)
It's my job....All living experiments
have to turn on their
creators...that's the rule....

KEN
Well, I'm going to put an end to
your rule...

Kelly enters the basement, visible. She's still a little
groggy.

KELLY
What's happening?

                    MARTIN
               (keeping eyes on T.V.)
          Sexual chaos is taking over the world
          and you made it with Ken while you
          were invisible.

                    KELLY
          Oh yeah. Sorry about that Ken. I
          just ouldn't control myself...

                    KEN
               (still strangling)
          I know because of this...this...
               (letting her go)
          I'm going to disinvent you. Uninvent
          you! There must be a way.

                    KELLY
               (to Ken)
          I did kinda enjoy it though.

                    KEN
               (to Kelly)
          What? Oh, yeah. Me too.

                    KELLY
          Maybe we can do it again sometime.

                    KEN
          Yeah. When we're both visible.

                    MARTIN
          True love. It's so romantic.

                    KELLY
               (smelling)
          Maybe we can do it again, now.

                    KEN
          Oh no. It's starting again. I wish
          we never invented you!

                    HORMONIOUS
          Sorry. I'm here to stay.

                    MARTIN
               (causally)
          Why don't you just go back in time
          and stop the invention from ever
          taking place?

Everyone and everything freezes for a second. They all look over at Martin who's still watching television.

KEN
(running over to light)
That's it! Can you do that?!! You said you can do anything! Can you sent me back in time one day to prevent the explosion that started it all?!

FLOATING LIGHT
You mean negative molecular deconstruction?

KEN
Yes! Wait....Do I?

FLOATING LIGHT
Time travel?

KEN
Right. Yes. Exactly!

KELLY
(rubbing against Ken)
We can do that!? Go back in time and change everything back to normal? Then you will be able to leave this planet because Hormonious would never have been invented to bring you here.

FLOATING LIGHT
That's right!

MARTIN
And everyone can live happily ever after.

KEN
Okay. I'm going. What do I have to do?

FLOATING LIGHT
Just destroy the chemicals before she mixes them together. That will counteract everything. Once the chemicals are destroyed, you will be returned to present time, we will disappear back to where we belong, and Hormonious will be undiscovered.

HORMONIOUS
And I was having such fun too.

KEN
(pushes Kelly off)
Kell, what exactly did you mix? Come on.
(MORE)

                    KEN (CONT'D)
          Try to control yourself for a couple
          of minutes. You accidentally heated
          up what?

                    KELLY:
               (gyrating her pelvis
                as she talks)
          Those bottles. The three multicolored
          things. They were on this table, I
          think. Or was it that table....Just
          let me take your clothes off!

                    KEN
               (holding her back)
          No, no, no. Kelly! You don't want to
          be like this all your life now. Just
          look at your pets!

Kelly looks over at the cages. All the rats and gerbils are
laying on their backs with their feet raised up, dead.

                    KEN (CONT'D)
          You see. They're dead! Dead from
          sexual exhaustion. And that's what's
          going to happen to you and everyone
          else if we don't stop it! Now think!
          Where were the bottles and when was
          the explosion?

                    KELLY
               (trying hard)
          I came down here at 7:45.
          Explosion..ten, fifteen minutes
          later.... Bottles...next to
          the...telescope, I think.

                    KEN
          Oh, great! I'm going to have to trash
          the entire room.

                    HORMONIOUS
          I'll go back with you. I know what
          I'm made up of. I guess, it's the
          least I can do.

                    KEN
          Okay. Fine. Now, what happens if I
          run into myself when I go back?

                    FLOATING LIGHT
          Can't happen. Can't happen.

                    MARTIN
               (holding Kelly)
          But what about that trilogy?

FLOATING LIGHT
They got it all wrong. Can't happen.
It's an impossible paradox. Two people
can't exist at the same place. The
same time range is pushing it already.
If you happen to run into yourself,
you just vanish until the area is
clear.

KEN
Okay. I got it. Send me back to...7:15
should be fine. 7:15 yesterday
morning, I break the bottles and...

FLOATING LIGHT
Everything will change. Only thing,
once we go away, it will be like we
were never here and all of the
adventures never happened. That's
means that you, Kelly, and your friend
there will go and do whatever would
have happened in the last day without
Hormonious and us around.

KEN
(confused)
That means?

FLOATING LIGHT
That you will be brought back to the
present time under an alternate set
of activities that happens within
the changed day. And you will have
no memory of us and Hormonious because
we never existed.

KEN
(still confused)
So, what are you saying?

FLOATING LIGHT
We have no control of where you will
reappear because the whole day will
have been changed. But don't worry,
you won't even notice because...

KEN
Is it just me or does this like make
no sense to anybody?

MARTIN
(still watching T.V.)
I tuned out a long time ago.

FLOATING LIGHT
What part didn't you understand? We
would be glad to repeat...

                    KEN
          Don't repeat! Just do it. Do it,
          okay?!

                    FLOATING LIGHT
          Right here? Right now?

                    KEN
          Yes.

                    HORMONIOUS
          No. Let's do it in the living room.
          This place was a mess yesterday. You
          don't want to be transported and
          find yourself stuck to the middle of
          a chair or table.

                    KEN
               (thinking)
          That makes a bit of sense. Okay.
          Upstairs! What do I have to do?

                    FLOATING LIGHT
          Just say ready and you're back.

                    KEN
          All right. Space light, it's been
          interesting. Kelly, Martin. See you
          someplace in the future when I get
          back. Hormonious, lets go!

                    KELLY
          Good luck.

Hormonious and Ken run upstairs. Martin holds Kelly back who's still squirming for Ken. Kelly squirms against Martin.

                    MARTIN(enjoying it)
          Oh, yes. That's very good.

                                        CUT TO:

INT. KELLY'S HOUSE - LIVING ROOM - EVENING.

Ken and Hormonious enter the living room. Ken takes a stand in the center of the room.

                    KEN
          Here good?

                    HORMONIOUS
               (smiling)
          Should be fine.

Suddenly Ken hears some sounds on the stairs. He looks up to see Jeff trying to crawl down the stairs.

                    JEFF
          Please, please...help...I can't walk
          anymore....

                    CHRISTIE
               (grabbing his feet)
          Come on back, lover!

Jeff is pulled back up the stairs. His hands reaching out
for help on the way up. His fingernails claw the walls on
the way up making marks.

                    JEFF (screaming)
          NOOO!!!

                    HORMONIOUS
          Poor guy.

                    KEN
          See what you've done.

                    HORMONIOUS
          What can I say? I'm good.

                    KEN
          Ready?

                    HORMONIOUS
          Ready.

                    KEN
          READY!!!

A strong beam of light shines up from the basement. The entire
room starts to glow red. Hormonious and Ken look at each
other.

Ken looks at his watch which starts winding backwards very
quickly.

What follows is a very sped-up scene of everything that has
happened in the last day in the living room, backwards. Ken
and Hormonious stand still during this TIME MONTAGE.

(Whenever "PAST KEN" enters the room backwards, "PRESENT
KEN" vanishes for the few seconds until "PAST KEN" leaves.)

This MONTAGE includes Jeff being pulled down the stairs and
then crawling back up.

Kelly walking backwards up the basement stairs through the
living room and up the main stairs.

"Past Ken" and Martin walking backwards up basement steps,
lifting invisible Kelly and then carrying her backwards
through front door.

The two European girls walking backwards into house, sitting on sofas and pulling out books.

Christie and Jeff run backwards down the stairs and straight through front door past the European girls on sofa.

The European girls closing books, getting up, walking backwards to kitchen and then leaving backwards through front door.

Kelly walking backwards from front door to basement.

Kelly's parents coming in backwards through front door, moving around, uneating their breakfast and then going back upstairs to sleep.

Kelly walking backwards from basement to the main stairs and up.

European girls enters through front door backwards, uneating breakfast, undressing, one goes backwards up the stairs, the other puts on her nightgown and lies down on the sofa to sleep, (a little midnight activity).

(SECOND DAY FROM NIGHT TO MORNING IS SIMILAR.) Should include European girls coming in backwards with bags and catching them as they fly up into their arms.

Jeff and Christie running in backwards from front door to basement as Christie continues to ungrab Jeff.

The girls walking backwards out front door with bags.

Jeff and Christie moving backwards from basement stairs to front door and out.

Ken entering house backwards covered with slime and walking across to basement stairs.

Kelly's mother running backwards down main stairs and down basement stairs, then backwards back up, picking up grocery bags and leaving through front door.

Ken and Kelly running across backwards from basement to front door and out.

Parents coming home backwards and going upstairs.

Christie coming home backwards and going up stairs.

Kelly coming home backwards and going into basement and then going upstairs.

European girls coming home backwards, undressing, putting on sexy nightgowns and going to sleep on sofas in living room.....

Everything starts to slow down as the clock turns back from nine, to eight, to 7:30, 7:25....7:20...7:16 and finally 7:15.

The red light disappears.

Ken and Hormonious is still standing in the living room. Ken shakes his head trying to register the last minute!

                    KEN(whispering) (CONT'D)
   I think we're here.

                    HORMONIOUS
     (yelling)
   That was fun!!!

The two European girls wake up at the sound. Ken tries to hush Hormonious up.

                    HORMONIOUS (CONT'D)
   Sorry, girls. Just try to ignore us.

                    MONIQUE
     (seeing Ken)
   What are you doing here?

                    KEN
   Me?...Oh, I'm just a dream. A very
   strange dream that is going to leave
   right now...

                    SHAWNEE
     (smelling and smiling)
   Never mind who you are. Why don't
   you join us?

                    KEN
   Oh no!

                  SHAWNEE & MONIQUE
   Oh yes!!!

They leap off the sofas in their skimpy nightgowns. Ken tries to run for the basement door. The two European girls cut him off.

Hormonious smiles and throws open the front door. As she runs out, she changes shape into a squirrel. The girls chase after Ken.

He runs around living room and then finally out the front door. The European girls follow him!

                                      CUT TO:

EXT. KELLY'S HOUSE AND STREET - MORNING - DAY BEFORE.

Ken is running down the street. The squirrel is running next to him and the girls are after him. MUSIC comes up.

> KEN(to squirrel)
> You planned this, didn't you? Part of a piece of furniture, my ass! You wanted this to happen!!

> HORMONIOUS
> I don't want to be nonexistent.

> KEN
> You're dead!

Ken dodges around a car that comes down the street. The girls continue to chase!

CUT TO:

EXT. KEN & HEMBURN'S HOUSE - MORNING.

Ken's car pulls up in Hemburn's driveway. Past Ken gets out and walks over to the front door.

> KEN(opening door) (CONT'D)
> Morning dogs. Ready to have a big filling breakfast.

Past Ken walks inside the house and closes the door behind him.

Sounds of screams, growls, and thuds come from inside the house.

> KEN(from inside house) (CONT'D)
> No! It's me!! Don't attack. DON'T ATTACK!!!!

CAMERA quickly pans from the Hemdale's house to across the street where Ken comes running out with squirrel and women chasing him!

Ken runs up his driveway and into his house. The squirrel jumps in just before Ken slams the door.

The European girls run up to the house and try to open the door.

CUT TO:

INT. KEN'S HOUSE - MORNING.

Ken is standing with his back to the door.

KEN (CONT'D)
These girls are determined.

Ken bolts the door shut. He can see from the glass in the door, Monique and Shawnee smiling and start stripping off their nightgowns. Ken then hears the squirrel giggling in the background. Ken turns to the squirrel with hatred in his eyes.

KEN (CONT'D)
You just came along to hijack the entire mission!?

HORMONIOUS
Hey, I'm your sex drive. I like to have fun.

KEN
Fun?...Fun!

HORMONIOUS
Ah-oh. I know this tone.

The squirrel turns and quickly hops upstairs. Ken chases after it.

KEN (chasing)
Come back here. It's dissecting time!!!

CUT TO:

INT. BASEMENT LAB - THE PRESENT - EVENING.

Martin is standing by the lab table. He lifts up the bowl of liquid Hormonious and sniffs it.

MARTIN
So, this is the stuff, huh?

KELLY
(not looking)
Uh-huh.

Kelly's eyes are fixed on the television. Her mouth wide open in awe. The television screen which was trying to avoid showing any real nudity on the screen is now focusing directly on the bouncing breasts and wiggling asses. In fact, the camera is chasing them around the room. Hormonious takes its affect on everyone.

STUDIO VOICE
What are you doing?! This is LIVE!!! Get back on Nancy! Nancy!!

Camera quickly shifts focus back to the on location news reporter, Nancy who is actually in the process of stripping off her clothes.

She smiles and quickly heads over to the camera which focuses directly on her breasts.

>   NANCY
>   Drop that camera, Fred and take off
>   your pants!!

CAMERA is dropped. It hits the floor of the gym and lays on its side still filming.

Martin walks over with bowl. He looks over Kelly's shoulder at the television.

>   MARTIN
>   And they say, there's nothing good
>   on television anymore.

                                                    CUT TO:

INT. KEN'S BEDROOM - DAY BEFORE.

The squirrel runs in and across the room. Ken is right behind. He grabs his baseball bat that's on the floor. The squirrel stops in front of a mirror and looks back, catching its breath. Ken spots it.

>   KEN
>   AHA!!

Ken throws the bat at the squirrel. The squirrel leaps away. The bat smashes into the mirror!

                                                    CUT TO:

INT. BASEMENT LAB - THE PRESENT - EVENING.

The television station cuts to color bars as a studio voice speaks.

>   STUDIO VOICE
>   We seemed to have lost contact with
>   our crew down at Jackson High...The
>   sex wave seems to be spreading through
>   the downtown area. The situation is
>   completely out of control...

Just then the basement door flies open. Jeff stumbles in. His clothes are ripped to shreds!

>   JEFF
>   She's gonna kill me! She's gonna
>   kill me! I can't take it anymore!

Kelly jumps up as Christie barges in. She is wearing a g-string and nothing else. Martin's eyes widen.

                  CHRISTIE
Where are you going, loverboy?

                    JEFF
        (running behind table)
She's possessed! Get a sexorcist!

Christie runs after Jeff. They run around the table. Martin looks at them and then back at the bowl. He grins

                    KELLY
God. I hope Ken can do it.

Christie corners Jeff. She is about to pounce when she smells the air. Christie cocks her head up.

Kelly sniffs too. She also turns her head. Both Kelly and Christie focus their attention on Martin, who is finishing rubbing some of liquid Hormonious on his neck.

                KELLY (CONT'D)
MARTIN! Don't!

                    MARTIN
The man needed help. I'm here to
help. Besides, can't let this stuff
go completely to waste.

Christie turns and approaches Martin. Kelly also is drawn closer but tries to resist. Martin smiles wide.

              MARTIN(to Kelly) (CONT'D)
Don't worry. When Ken destroys the
chemicals, none of what we're about
to do will have ever happened.

                    KELLY
        (moving forwards)
But what if he fails?

                    MARTIN
I can live with that too.

Kelly and Christie tackle Martin and begin ripping his clothes off. Martin doesn't struggle.

Jeff slowly gets up from his corner. He looks over at them and shrugs as he regains his breath. He then glances up and spots the floating space light. He jumps back slightly.

             FLOATING LIGHT(to Jeff)
Hello.

                    JEFF
               (baffled)
          Hi.

                    FLOATING LIGHT
          Would you like us to increase your
          sexual stamina?

                    JEFF
               (after a pause)
          Maybe later.

                                                       CUT TO:

INT. KEN'S BEDROOM - MORNING (PAST).

The squirrel darts into the closet. Ken grabs the bat and jumps up.

                    KEN
          You're really starting to piss me
          off now!!

Suddenly the door to Ken's bedroom bursts open. Monique and Shawnee, wearing nothing but their underwear run into the room.

                    KEN (CONT'D)
          Oh, shit!

Ken runs into the closet and slams the door behind him!

                                                       CUT TO:

EXT. HEMBURN'S HOUSE - MORNING (PAST).

Past Ken runs out the front door and slams it behind him. He fixes his hair and clothes.

                    PAST KEN
          I hate those dogs.

Past Ken takes a breath and starts back to his car that's in the Hemburn driveway.

                                                       CUT TO:

INT./EXT. GYM - NIGHT - (THE PRESENT).

MUSIC starts up as VIDEO CAMERAS shoot everything and everyone going crazy. There are quick clips of people having sex in the park, sex in doorways, sex in the swimming pools. People is various stages of undress are running rampant. It's a full scale orgy.

CAMERA pans with naked bodies running across the street chasing each other and shifts over to a new newsman standing by with a microphone.

                    NEWS PERSON(trying to stay calm)
        Riots are breaking out everywhere.
        Amazingly only few cases of sexual
        assault have been reported. And one
        Jackson High student has this to
        say:

The news person turns to a half-dressed male student.

                    STUDENT(taped)
        I'm telling you the truth! The whole
        thing started because of this big,
        huge octopus!

                                            CUT TO:

EXT. KEN'S HOUSE - MORNING (PAST).

Ken is climbing down the ladder. His shirt is pulled off by Monique and Shawnee. They scream after him.

Ken, without shirt, leaps down last rungs and runs around the house.

                                            CUT TO:

EXT. ROAD - MORNING. (PAST).

Past Ken pulls the car out of the driveway, hits the gas, and drives quickly down the road.

Ken runs out in front of the car. Ken, in road freezes, as he sees his car head right for him! Suddenly, Ken disappears. The car drives right past where he was standing, continues on, and turns the corner.

As soon as the car is out of view, Ken reappears in the middle of the street exactly as before. He is frozen for a second. He looks around for the car, and realizes he's okay.

                    KEN
        Now, I understand. Damn good thing I
        was driving.

Ken looks to the side and sees Monique and Shawnee burst out of his house.

                  KEN (CONT'D)
        Oh, man. This has got to end!

He starts to run down the street again when a car pulls up next to him. Dan and his group are in the car.

                    DAN
          Well, get a load of this.
                    (notices the naked
                     girls)
          Holy mother...!

Ken opens the door and squeezes into the car. Monique and
Shawnee run over. Ken slams door and locks it.

                    KEN
          Just drive! Drive, Dan. Please!

                    DAN
          Wait just a second here. I think
          these ladies would like to have a
          ride. Guys, would you like to let
          the girls in?

                    KEN
          No. Don't open the doors!

                    DAN
          What are you, out of your fuckin'
          mind?!

Monique and Shawnee start pounding on the car doors and
windows. Their breasts press up against the car. All the
boys are staring and drooling.

                    KEN
          Look, they're friendly, beautiful,
          and... Well, remember the big twist
          in "The Crying Game"?

                    ALL THE GUYS
                    (changes expression,
                     screaming)
          SHIT!!!!

The car skids off down the road, leaving the girls standing
there.

                                                  CUT TO:

INT. DAN'S CAR - MORNING.

The five guys and Ken are crowded in.

                    KEN
          Thanks a lot, Dan.

                    DAN
          No, thank-you for that warning. Man,
          I should have guessed it. I mean,
          they really looked desperate. That
          was too close. Just the thought gives
          me the chills.

                    KEN
          Well, thanks anyway.
              (looks at watch, 7:33.)
          Shit. Dan, I know this is asking a
          lot but I really need you to drop me
          off at Kelly's. Listen, I'm really
          sorry about the science experiment
          and everything but this is a matter
          of life and...

                    DAN
          What about the experiment? There's
          something wrong with the one you
          made for me? That's right. The
          accident hasn't happened yet.

                    KEN
          Ah,...yeah. Yes there is. It doesn't
          work. Don't try it. It's some stupid
          jogging thing. When I get to school,
          you can have mine instead. It's a
          plant protector. It works great. I
          have to pick it up at Kelly's though.

                    DAN
              (thinking and turning)
          All right. This better get me an A.
          Cause you know what will happen if I
          don't get an A.

All the guys in the back seat make a fist and hit their other hands in a threatening way.

                    KEN
          Don't worry. You will. No doubt about
          it. Just don't use the jogging
          reducer. No-Matter-what-I- say, don't
          use the jogger.

                    DAN
          What are you talking about? You are
          fuckin' weird.

                    KEN
          I know. I know.

                                        CUT TO:

EXT. KELLY'S HOUSE - MORNING.

Dan's car pulls up. Ken hops out.

                    KEN (CONT'D)
          Thanks. Meet you at school in a couple
          of seconds.

                    DAN
          Seconds?

                    KEN
               (running to house)
          Don't worry. I'll be there.

Dan drives off. Ken runs to front door as it starts to open.
Ken quickly cuts around to the back of the house as Mr. and
Mrs. Brown walk out.

                                                  CUT TO:

EXT. KELLY'S BACKYARD - MORNING.

Ken runs around looking at watch; 7:39. Ken looks up and
stops short. He then slowly reaches his hand out to feel the
air around him. He moves forward, trying to feel something.

Female Hormonious appears in the basement window.

                    HORMONIOUS (from window)
          Hey, dummy. They haven't landed yet,
          remember?

                    KEN
               (dropping hands)
          I knew that.

Ken climbs in the window.

                                                  CUT TO:

INT. BASEMENT LAB - MORNING.

Ken drops to the floor.

                    KEN (CONT'D)
          I've got four minutes. Which ones?

                    HORMONIOUS
          Well, let me see now....

                    KEN
          Oh, go screw yourself!

                    HORMONIOUS
          Hmmm, I wonder if I could do that.

Ken moves to destroy the place and Hormonious.

                    HORMONIOUS (CONT'D)
          Okay, okay...I'm kidding. Sorry.
          It's those bottles.

Hormonious points to the three multi-colored bottles on the
counter next to the computer.

                        KEN
                (starting to move for
                 them)
            Wait. Why should I trust you? An out-
            of-control mistake?!

                        HORMONIOUS
                    (moving towards him)
            I may be playful but I'm not really
            destructive. I can see that your
            world isn't ready for me yet. Sex
            has its place and time and I'm aware
            of that now.

                        KEN
            A sex drive with a conscience?

                        HORMONIOUS
            You do good work, creator, and you
            weren't too far off. But I suggest
            dropping the project. Like I said,
            don't fool with mother nature. She
            can get pissed off too. Things tend
            to take care of themselves.

She hands Ken the three bottles but doesn't let go. Ken looks up at her.

                        HORMONIOUS (CONT'D)
            One last kiss before I go?...Please.

Ken leans in and puckers up. Hormonious leans in. They kiss lightly until Hormonious reaches around and grabs Ken. She plants a big major kiss on his lips. When they break, Ken is speechless. Hormonious smiles.

                        HORMONIOUS (CONT'D)
            I'll always be with you.
                    (points to his forehead)
            Right here.
                    (slowly backs away
                     into the corner)
            Now drop it.

Hormonious quickly backs up into the corner of the basement she came out from and braces herself for the explosion.

                        HORMONIOUS (CONT'D)
            See you around....
                    (Ken looks at her
                     with concern)
            ...the floor.

Ken smiles, raises the bottles over his head, and the basement door swings open.

Kelly enters and stops short when she sees Ken.

                    KELLY
          What are you doing here?!

                    KEN
               (thinking and then
                smiling)
          I'm not here.

Ken drops the bottles to the floor. They crash against the
ground and shatter. A burst of smoke shoots up!

                                                  CUT TO:

A SERIES OF QUICK CUTS of various scenes freezing in mid-
action. Each freeze is followed by a quick flash of light!

1) Various people having sex in the streets.

2) Various students in the gym stripping off their clothes.

3) Various teen-agers on washing machines, coffee tables, in
bathrooms, on statues, with vibrators...(you get the picture).

4) Slime shooting out of the octopus tentacles.

5) Ms. Puddle and the nurse chasing Ken around the room.

6) Martin, Kelly, and Christie rolling around the basement
floor.

7) The liquid flowing out of the bowl.

8) And finally the space light shooting away, out the window
and back into space.

As the red glow disappears from the dish and a beam of light
shoots back into the sky, one can barely hear;

                    FLOATING LIGHT
          Bye, Kelly.

9) Past Kelly watches as the smoke clears. Ken has indeed
vanished.

10) Martin, Kelly, and Christie are on the floor. Kelly is
down to her bra and underpants. She's kissing Martin's face.
Christie is naked on top of Martin. Martin is loving every
minute.

                    MARTIN(in ecstasy)
          YES! THAT'S IT! I'M GONNA...I'M
          GONNA...!!

Suddenly, they all vanish from the basement, leaving it empty.
CAMERA quickly zooms over to a clock on the wall: 7:45 p.m.

                                              FLASH CUT TO:

INT. BASEMENT LAB - NIGHT (ALTERNATE AND NOW REAL PRESENT).

CAMERA is still tight on clock which just turns to 7:45 p.m.

CAMERA pulls back to Martin, Kelly, and Ken They are all fully clothed and the only ones in the room. Kelly is sweeping up the broken glass. Ken is mixing together something by the lab tables.

Martin is talking.

                    KELLY(laughing)
Tell me. Tell me. Ken refused to talk about it.

                    MARTIN
Well, Ken puts on the jogging belt and before anyone knows what's going on, the thing has ripped off his shirt...

                    KELLY
Oh no?!

                    KEN
Martin, I would really like to forget...

                    MARTIN
But that's not the good part. He then tilts it down and rips off Ms. Puddle's skirt too!

                    KELLY
Get out of here!?

                    MARTIN
Lost his teacher's aid job! Hey, but you're lucky. If Dan hadn't forced you to trade projects and it had happened to him... Whoa! I would want to be you now.

                    KEN
Yeah, I'm so lucky. First the Auto jog heat reducer backfires, then Kelly destroys the hormone experiment...

                    KELLY
I saw you drop these bottles. At least, I thought I saw you...

                    KEN
Right. I was here and at school at the same time...!

                    MARTIN
          Relax, Bud. It was a stupid project
          anyway. Start a new experiment.
          Figure out a way to physically remove
          women's clothes. Or get into other
          people's bodies and have sex with
          them. Or how about a development
          serum that increases the size of
          your sex organs? Just think Kelly,
          hooters out to here!

                    KELLY
          You're disgusting.

                    KEN
          Well, for once you may be right,
          Martin. Something keeps telling me
          that the hormone project was a
          mistake. However, this idea is certain
          not to fail.

                    MARTIN
          What now? Asexual reproduction?

                    KEN
          No. Dreams. I think all of our
          problems and all of the answers can
          be found in our dreams.

                    MARTIN
          So?

                    KELLY
              (holds up a potion)
          So, with the right mixture to enhance
          brainwave activity, Ken and I think
          that we can hook up a person's mental
          dreams to a television screen and...

                    KEN
              (placing two electrodes
               on his head)
          Presto! Mental movies from the mind.

                                        SMASH CUT TO:

INT. BASEMENT LAB - A BIT LATER.

Ken is asleep on a cot in the corner. Two electrodes are
attached to his head. The wires run out and into the back of
the television set. Kelly checks Ken's pulse. Martin is seated
in front of the screen. Kelly walks over to him.

                    KELLY
          He's asleep. Let's turn it on and
          see what we get.

                          MARTIN
                Have any popcorn?

Kelly turns on the television and sits down next to Martin.
The screen is full of static for a few seconds.

                          MARTIN (CONT'D)
                Looking into the mind of Ken Ashbrook.
                Now, there's a scary thought.

C.U. of the television screen as Hormonious' head pops up in
front of the static. She looks directly towards Martin and
Kelly.

                          HORMONIOUS
                You ain't seen nothing yet! Come on
                in. Join the party.

Hormonious points at them. A beam of light shoots out of the
television screen! It hits Martin and Kelly. They suddenly
vanish!

Kelly and Martin suddenly appear inside the television screen!
They look around, confused.

                          MARTIN(inside television)
                Kelly?! What's happening? What did
                you do?

Hormonious pops up behind them inside the television screen.

                          HORMONIOUS
                Hi, guys. Ever hear the expression;
                "Mind over matter"?

Hormonious suddenly rips off all of her clothes. She stands
naked behind them. Kelly and Martin look at her and then at
each other.

                          HORMONIOUS (CONT'D)
                Let the wet dreams begin!

Kelly and Martin scream and run away. Hormonious laughs and
looks directly at the screen from inside.

                          HORMONIOUS(to CAMERA) (CONT'D)
                Freddy Kruger. Eat your heart out.

Hormonious smiles and winks. The television screen suddenly
shuts off.

                                              QUICK FADE OUT: